Lecture Notes in Computer Science 15426

Founding Editors

Gerhard Goos
Juris Hartmanis

The series Lecture Notes in Computer Science (LNCS), including its subseries Lecture Notes in Artificial Intelligence (LNAI) and Lecture Notes in Bioinformatics (LNBI), has established itself as a medium for the publication of new developments in computer science and information technology research, teaching, and education.

LNCS enjoys close cooperation with the computer science R & D community, the series counts many renowned academics among its volume editors and paper authors, and collaborates with prestigious societies. Its mission is to serve this international community by providing an invaluable service, mainly focused on the publication of conference and workshop proceedings and postproceedings. LNCS commenced publication in 1973.

Ruifeng Xu · Huan Chen · Yirui Wu ·
Liang-Jie Zhang
Editors

Cognitive Computing - ICCC 2024

8th International Conference
Held as Part of the Services Conference Federation, SCF 2024
Bangkok, Thailand, November 16–19, 2024
Proceedings

 Springer

Editors
Ruifeng Xu 🆔
Harbin Institute of Technology
Harbin, China

Huan Chen
SF Technology Co., Ltd.
Shenzhen, China

Yirui Wu
Hohai University
Nanjing, China

Liang-Jie Zhang 🆔
Shenzhen University
Shenzhen, China

ISSN 0302-9743   ISSN 1611-3349 (electronic)
Lecture Notes in Computer Science
ISBN 978-3-031-77953-4   ISBN 978-3-031-77954-1 (eBook)
https://doi.org/10.1007/978-3-031-77954-1

Preface

The 2024 International Conference on Cognitive Computing (ICCC) aimed to cover all aspects of Sensing Intelligence (SI) as a Service (SIaaS). Cognitive Computing is a sensing-driven-computing (SDC) scheme that explores and integrates intelligence from all types of senses in various scenarios and solution contexts. It goes well beyond the four normal human senses, which consist of four major senses (sight, smell, hearing, and taste) located in specific parts of the body, as well as a sense of touch located all over the body.

ICCC 2024 was a member of the Services Conference Federation (SCF). SCF 2024 had the following 10 collocated service-oriented sister conferences: 2024 International Conference on Web Services (ICWS 2024), 2024 International Conference on Cloud Computing (CLOUD 2024), 2024 International Conference on Services Computing (SCC 2024), 2024 International Conference on Big Data (BigData 2024), 2024 International Conference on AI and Multimodal Services (AIMS 2024), 2024 International Conference on Metaverse (METAVERSE 2024), 2024 International Conference on Internet of Things (ICIOT 2024), 2024 International Conference on Cognitive Computing (ICCC 2024), 2024 International Conference on Edge Computing (EDGE 2024), and 2024 International Conference on Blockchain (ICBC 2024).

This volume presents the accepted papers of the 2024 International Conference on Cognitive Computing (ICCC 2024), held in Bangkok, Thailand during November 16–19, 2024. For this conference, each paper was single-blind reviewed by three independent members of the International Program Committee. After carefully evaluating their originality and quality, we accepted 8 papers.

We are pleased to thank the authors whose submissions and participation made this conference possible. We also want to express our thanks to the Organizing Committee and Program Committee members, for their dedication in helping to organize the conference and reviewing the submissions. We owe special thanks to the keynote speakers for their impressive speeches.

Finally, we would like to thank operations team members Jing Zeng, Sheng He, Yishuang Ning, and Zhuolin Mei for their excellent work in organizing this conference. We look forward to your future great contributions as a volunteer, author, and conference participant in the fast-growing worldwide services innovations community.

September 2024

Ruifeng Xu
Huan Chen
Yirui Wu
Liang-Jie Zhang

Organization

Program Chairs

Ruifeng Xu	Harbin Institute of Technology, China
Huan Chen	SF Technology Co., Ltd., China
Yirui Wu	Hohai University, China

Services Conference Federation (SCF 2024)

General Chairs

Ali Arsanjani	Google, USA
Wu Chou	Essenlix Corporation, USA

Coordinating Program Chair

Liang-Jie Zhang	Shenzhen University, China

CFO and International Affairs Chair

Min Luo	Georgia Tech, USA

Operation Committee

Jing Zeng	China Gridcom Co., Ltd., China
Yishuang Ning	Tsinghua University, China
Sheng He	Kingdee International Software Group Co., Ltd., China
Zhuolin Mei	Jiujiang University, China

Steering Committee

Calton Pu (Co-chair)	Georgia Tech, USA
Liang-Jie Zhang (Co-chair)	Shenzhen University, China

ICCC 2024 Program Committee

Nagarajan Kandasamy	Drexel University, USA
Supratik Mukhopadhyay	Louisiana State University, USA
Yi Zhou	University of Science and Technology Beijing, China
Liuqing Chen	Zhejiang University, China
Yong Lu	Minzu University of China, China
Dong Wen	University of Science and Technology Beijing, China
Min Lu	Shenzhen University, China
Ye Liu	Institute of Psychology, University of Chinese Academy of Sciences, China
Peng Xu	Northeast Normal University, China
M. Emre Gürsoy	Koç University, Turkey
Carson Leung	University of Manitoba, Canada
Jing Zeng	China Gridcom Co., Ltd., China
Limin Su	Beijing Union University, China
Dwith Chenna	Magic Leap, USA

Conference Sponsor – Services Society

The Services Society (S2) is a non-profit professional organization that has been created to promote worldwide research and technical collaboration in services innovations among academia and industrial professionals. Its members are volunteers from industry and academia with common interests. S2 is registered in the USA as a "501(c) organization", which means that it is an American tax-exempt nonprofit organization. S2 collaborates with other professional organizations to sponsor or co-sponsor conferences and to promote an effective services curriculum in colleges and universities. S2 initiates and promotes a "Services University" program worldwide to bridge the gap between industrial needs and university instruction.

The Services Sector accounted for 79.5% of the GDP of the USA in 2016. The Services Society has formed 5 Special Interest Groups (SIGs) to support technology- and domain-specific professional activities.

- Special Interest Group on Services Computing (SIG-SC)
- Special Interest Group on Big Data (SIG-BD)
- Special Interest Group on Cloud Computing (SIG-CLOUD)
- Special Interest Group on Artificial Intelligence (SIG-AI)
- Special Interest Group on Metaverse (SIG-Metaverse)

About Services Conference Federation (SCF)

As the founding member of the Services Conference Federation (SCF), the first **International Conference on Web Services (ICWS)** was held in June 2003 in Las Vegas, USA. Meanwhile, the First International Conference on Web Services - Europe 2003 (ICWS-Europe 2003) was held in Germany in October 2003. ICWS-Europe 2003 was an extended event of the 2003 International Conference on Web Services (ICWS 2003) in Europe. In 2004, ICWS-Europe was changed to the European Conference on Web Services (ECOWS), which was held at Erfurt, Germany. Sponsored by the Services Society and Springer, SCF 2018 and SCF 2019 were held successfully in Seattle and San Diego, USA. SCF 2020 and SCF 2021 were held successfully online and in Shenzhen, China. SCF 2022 and 2023 were held successfully in Hawaii, USA. To celebrate its 22nd birthday, SCF 2024 was held on November 16–19, 2024, in Bangkok, Thailand.

In the past 21 years, the ICWS community has expanded from Web engineering innovations to scientific research for the whole services industry. Service delivery platforms have been expanded to mobile platforms, Internet of Things, cloud computing, and edge computing. The services ecosystem has gradually been enabled, value added, and intelligence embedded through enabling technologies such as big data, artificial intelligence, and cognitive computing. In the coming years, all transactions with multiple parties involved will be transformed to blockchain.

Based on technology trends and best practices in the field, the Services Conference Federation (SCF) will continue serving as the conference umbrella's code name for all services-related conferences. SCF 2024 defined the future of New ABCDE (AI, Blockchain, Cloud, BigData & IOT) and entered the 5G for Services Era. The theme of ICWS 2024 was Web-based Services for Metaverse Era. We are very proud to announce that SCF 2024's 10 co-located theme topic conferences all centered around "services", with each focusing on exploring different themes (web-based services, cloud-based services, Big Data-based services, services innovation lifecycle, AI-driven ubiquitous services, blockchain-driven trust service ecosystems, industry-specific services and applications, and emerging service-oriented technologies).

- Bigger Platform: The 10 collocated conferences (SCF 2024) were sponsored by the Services Society, which is the world-leading not-for-profit organization (501(c)(3)) dedicated to the service of more than 30,000 worldwide Services Computing researchers and practitioners. A bigger platform means bigger opportunities for all volunteers, authors, and participants. Meanwhile, Springer provided sponsorship of the best paper awards and other professional activities. All the 10 conference proceedings of SCF 2024 were published by Springer and indexed in the ISI Conference Proceedings Citation Index (included in Web of Science), Engineering Index EI (Compendex and Inspec databases), DBLP, Google Scholar, IO-Port, MathSciNet, Scopus, and ZBlMath.
- Brighter Future: While celebrating the 2024 version of ICWS, SCF 2024 highlighted the International Conference on AI and Multimodal Services (AIMS 2024) to build

the fundamental infrastructure for enabling AIGC services ecosystems. It will also lead our community members to create their own brighter future.

- Better Model: SCF 2024 continued to leverage the invented Conference Blockchain Model (CBM) to innovate the organizing practices for all the 10 theme conferences. Senior researchers in the field are welcome to submit proposals to serve as CBM Ambassador for an individual conference to start better interactions during your leadership role in organizing future SCF conferences.

Contents

Research Track

A Review of Link Prediction on Heterogeneous Networks

Rui Mi[1], Changbo Wang[2], Liang-Jie Zhang[3], Yirui Wu[4], Junyang Chen[3(✉)], and Huan Wang[1]

[1] College of Informatics, Huazhong Agricultural University, Wuhan, China
mirui2023@webmail.hzau.edu.cn, hwang@mail.hzau.edu.cn
[2] Center of Health Administration and Development Studies,
Hubei University of Medicine, Shiyan, China
[3] College of Computer Science and Software Engineering, Shenzhen University,
Shenzhen, China
zhanglj@ieee.org, junyangchen@szu.edu.cn
[4] Hohai University, Nanjing, China
wuyirui@hhu.edu.cn

Abstract. Link prediction is a central downstream assignment in network analysis, which denotes an attempt to assess the probability of a connection between two nodes based on observed link and node properties, which can be utilized across diverse categories of graph system, including knowledge graphs, network traffic, social networks, biological networks, etc. Heterogeneous networks usually contain diverse nodes and a variety of edges' type, which can preserve more information than homogeneous information networks. However, the majority of researches focus on graph representation analysis of homogeneous networks. Limited research has systematically reviewed advanced techniques for link prediction and applications on Heterogeneous Information Networks (HIN). Building upon this, we propose a classification summary for link prediction methods in heterogeneous information graphs. We will introduce some classical methods and some newly proposed methods for link prediction on heterogeneous graphs. We provide general technical ideas behind each method in classes and analysis performance of models. We further discuss the applications of link prediction on complex heterogeneous graphs across various domains. Additionally, the research challenges are discussed, and several possible research avenues for link prediction on heterogeneous network are pointed out.

Keywords: heterogeneous networks · graph analysis · link prediction

1 Introduction

Link prediction in graph networks refers to predicting missing links which may be due to omissions during data collection or errors during transmission, or predicting potential links [1]. Link prediction is a widely used downstream task in recommendation systems [2], medicine interactions [3], etc. A huge number of link

© The Author(s), under exclusive license to Springer Nature Switzerland AG 2025
R. Xu et al. (Eds.): ICCC 2024, LNCS 15426, pp. 3–19, 2025.
https://doi.org/10.1007/978-3-031-77954-1_1

prediction methods on homogeneous networks have been proposed, where the main idea is to analyze the similarities and connection patterns between nodes. However, most real networks contain diverse nodes types or relation between nodes [4], which opens up a new research topic called heterogeneous networks. In such networks, most of the link prediction models proposed based on homogeneous complex graphs are not suitable for heterogeneous complex graphs. In response to the above traits, researchers have proposed many heterogeneous networks link prediction algorithms, such as meta-path methods [5], methods based on graph embedding [6] and graph neural network [7] which effectively capture relationships and semantic information between nodes, emerging as a prominent research area in recent years.

However, existing methods for link prediction in heterogeneous graphs still faces several challenges. For example, data sparsity [8] and noise [9] in heterogeneous networks also have an impact on link prediction accuracy, which needs further research; The semantic correlation between original nodes needs preservation in the process of link prediction [10]. Recently, novel issues continue to emerge in this filed, such as dynamic heterogeneous network link prediction [1] and few-shot learning [8] for link prediction on heterogeneous information graphs.

Few studies have systematically reviewed the most advanced link prediction techniques and applications only in heterogeneous networks. Based on this, This article conducts a comprehensive survey of link prediction on heterogeneous networks, containing traditional and novel strategies, applications in various fields. In summary, the major contributions in this article can be outlined as follows:

- A taxonomy of link prediction on heterogeneous graphs is proposed, in which methods are divided into six categories.
- We provide comprehensive overview of link prediction techniques only focusing on heterogeneous networks. We also collect practical applications for link prediction in various domains.
- We identify the limitations of existing methods for link prediction on heterogeneous graphs. Additionally, we propose novel research directions to overcome these challenges.

2   Notations and Definitions

We provide a set of commonly used notations and present some critical definitions which will be used in this paper. Specifically, matrices are denoted by bold uppercase characters, while vectors are denoted by bold lowercase characters in this paper. The notations which will be mentioned are illustrated in Table 1. Then, some definitions are introduced in the following.

Definition 1. *Heterogeneous Graph: A Heterogeneous graph $G = (V, E, A, L)$ consists of a node set $V = \{v_1, v_2, \ldots, v_n\}$. Any two node types A_1, A_2 determine the only one edge type. In this paper, different connections should be established depending on the specific node type. A graph may have node attributes $\boldsymbol{X} = \{x_1, x_2, \ldots, x_n\}$, where $x_i \in R^d$ representing the feature vector of node v_i.*

Similarly, the set of hyperedges in hypergraph is denoted as $E = \{e_1, \ldots, e_N\}$ and $e_i = \{e \in E \mid v_i \in e\}$ connects more than two nodes.

Definition 2. *Link Prediction : Link prediction models tend to predict missing or potential links while determine the type of links in heterogeneous networks. Given a heterogeneous graph G, for any two nodes v_1, v_2 given arbitrarily in G, Link prediction tasks analyze and mine the structure and characteristics of these heterogeneous networks, and calculate similarities or other characteristics between nodes denoted as $p(i, j)$ that determine the probability of the existence of the edge which connects nodes v_1 and v_2.*

Table 1. Commonly Used Notations

Notations	Descriptions
$e_{i,j}$	An edge $e_{i,j} \in E$.
$N(v)$	The neighbors of a node v.
$\mathbf{A}$	The adjacency matrix of graph.
$\mathbf{D}$	The degree matrix of $\mathbf{A}$.
$\mathbf{Z}$	The common latent space of $\mathbf{A}$.
m	Edges number, $m = |E|$.
d	The dimension of feature embedding.
c	The seen classes.
$X \in R^{n \times d}$	The feature matrix of a graph.
$x_v \in R^d$	The feature vector of the node v.
k	The layer index.
$\sigma(\cdot)$	The sigmoid activation function.
$\mathbf{W}, \Theta, w, \theta, b$	Learnable parameters.
$\mathcal{L}$	A loss function.
$\odot$	Element-wise multiplication operation.
$\mathcal{N}(\cdot)$	A Gaussian distribution function.
$t(v)$	Node type v.
$r(e)$	The type of relation of edge e.
$AL(v_1)$	The list of all possible nodes for node v_1
$p(i, j)$	The probability that node v_1 meeting node v_2

3   Link Prediction Methods on Heterogeneous Networks

Link prediction strategies in heterogeneous information graphs have attracted notice recently, where the types of nodes or edges are different, which makes difficulties to deal with. In this section, we categorize link prediction methods on heterogeneous networks into six aspects. Several popular algorithms of each category are introduced.

3.1 Methods Based on Unsupervised Learning

In heterogeneous network link prediction, unsupervised methods refer to methods that do not require labeled data for prediction. These methods usually rely on the traits of nodes and edges and exploit these characteristics to infer unknown links . Because labeled data is not usually abundant, unsupervised methods may suffer from complexity and data noise in most cases [4].

The simplest form of heterogeneous networks is bipartite graph which refers to a graph consisting of two distinct types of nodes, with edges connecting nodes of different types only. However, the common neighbor methods, which are triangle-based, require modification to be applicable in bipartite networks. Davis *et al.* [4] extend unique path (s, n, t) of length two from node s to node t belonging to common neighbor n, to length three, and formulate bipartite Jaccard's coefficient where unique paths of length three are shared between two nodes, extending common neighbors link prediction to bipartite network, by the total number of unique paths of length three starting from either s or t. They also change the expression of Adamic/Adar to expression as $log(\mid N_{n1} \mid + \mid N_{n2} \mid)$. However, strategies above are not applicable to heterogeneous networks by nature which contains different types of nodes and edges, and even complex association patterns. The measures need to be redefined with utilization of weight information for extension to heterogeneous networks. A novel probabilistically weighted extension of the Adamic/Adar measure for heterogeneous information networks [4] proposes a suitable weighting scheme that considers the different combinations of edge types. This weighting scheme serves as a weighted extension of neighborhood methods. Davis *et al.* also propose a supervised learning models called MR-HPLP which uses random forests [11] within each bag [12], and then composes a separate amalgam of features from each of the other homogeneous projections for training. In comparing the results of two methods, they find unsupervised link predictors can still exhibit domain-specific limitations and lack flexibility, which is not good as supervised methods.

3.2 Methods Based on Machine Learning

Machine learning (ML) approaches have been widely adopted for link prediction tasks in heterogeneous networks mainly contain random forest, support vector machines, decision trees, matrix factorization, etc. Projected Metric Embedding PME [13] aimming to heterogeneous information networks embeddings can capture both first-order and second-order proximities simultaneously. It first maps the nodes from the original node space to the corresponding relationship space. It then calculates the similarity between projected nodes in the relationship space based on Euclidean distance, where the scoring function is denoted as:

$$f_r(v_i, v_j) = w_{ij} \|\mathbf{M_r}\mathbf{v_i} - \mathbf{M_r}\mathbf{v_j}\|, r \in \mathcal{R} \tag{1}$$

where $\mathbf{M_r}\mathbf{v_i}$ denotes the projected vector representation for node v_i and $\|\mathbf{M_r}\mathbf{v_i} - \mathbf{M_r}\mathbf{v_j}\|$ denotes the distance between node v_i and v_j in r-relation space.

This similarity not only measures distance, but also has semantic information. It then performs negative sampling from both ends of an edge and utilizes loss-aware adaptive sampling method for model optimization. HEER [14] studies the problem of comprehensive transcription on heterogeneous networks which can learn the representations of the input heterogeneous information graph that retains the rich information as comprehensively as possible and do not require additional expertise or feature engineering. It utilizes edge representations and heterogeneous metrics to perform graph embedding. As ML is widely applied in homogeneous graphs, ongoing advancements and the integration of various techniques are likely to enhance model effectiveness.

3.3   Methods Based on Deep Learning

Graph neural networks (GNNs) are a type of deep learning model specifically designed for graph-structured data, which have shown superior performance as it can combine both structures and attribute information for graph data [15]. We widely divide the methods based on deep learning (DL) into DL with random walk, metapath based and others. By analyzing the collected information from the random walks, methods on heterogeneous networks analysis can estimate the likelihood of relation between two nodes [16]. The assumption is that if two nodes have similar attributes, are connected to similar types of nodes, and have similar neighbors, they are more likely to have a trust relationship. HetGNN [17] employed a random walk algorithm to sample a fixed number of correlated heterogeneous neighbors for each node. These neighbors are then grouped based on their respective node types. Then it designs a neural network framework to encode heterogeneous contents embeddings for nodes and then aggregate content embeddings of different neighboring types. Finally, to effectively train the model and optimize its performance, it employ a graph content loss and utilize a mini-batch gradient descent procedure.

A meta-path M is denoted in the state of $A_1 \xrightarrow{R_1} A_2 \xrightarrow{R_2} \ldots \xrightarrow{R_l} A_{l+1}$, which denotes the sequence of object types A_1 and A_{l+1}, and relations R connecting them, which has been widely used to mine semantic information in heterogeneous networks [18]. Heterogeneous graph neural networks for link prediction usually fuse information from different metapaths, which follow two steps: utilize single meta-path to aggregate neighbors and then utilize multiple meta-paths to aggregate rich semantics. For example, HAGNN [19] integrates two aggregation techniques for meta-path-based intra-type and meta-path-free inter-type. These techniques are combined to effectively aggregate information within the same type of nodes based on meta-paths and across different types of nodes without relying on specific meta-paths. During the phase of intra-type aggregation, HAGNN utilizes a fused meta-path network to capture the neighbors within a specific meta-path of a given node type. The structural semantic weight, represented by the number of path containing nodes and edges, is considered for aggregating structural semantic information. HGT [20] achieves efficient prediction capabilities by learning the representation vectors of nodes and edges and using a self-attention mechanism to efficiently capture the relations between nodes, which is based on GNN and Transformer structure to model heterogeneous graph data. Different from traditional hierarchical approaches capturing rich semantics which simply exploits structural characteristics and usually omits node content features, MAGNN [21] is introduced to resolve these limitations, which consists of three main components. Firstly, it applies type-specific linear transformations to the input node attributes to capture the node content effectively. Secondly, it utilizes the attention mechanism [22] during the intra-metapath aggregation, where the intermediate semantic nodes are merged which can obtain more informative embeddings. Lastly, it combines messages from multiple metapaths during the inter-metapath aggregation to generate the final node embeddings. A Topic-aware Heterogeneous Graph Neural Network (THGNN) [23] hierarchically mines topic-aware semantics from learning rich unstructured text content of node which is latent but more finegrained than structural semantics for link prediction. In its intrametapath decomposition mechanism, it applies a multi-facet transformation matrix where the features of different types of nodes are projected into the fine-grained topic-aware semantics relying on the global knowledge from unstructured text content in heterogeneous networks. The metapath-specific multi-facet k^{th} topic-aware representation of target node u denotes as:

$$\mathbf{h}_{u,k}^{M_i} = L2\_Norm \left(\sum_{c \in C_u^{M_i}} p_{k|c_u} \cdot f \left(\{ h_{v,k}, \forall v \in c_u \} \right) \right), \qquad (2)$$

where $k = 1, 2, \ldots, K$, $c_u \in C_u^{M_i}$ indicates sampled metapath M_i-based contexts for u and $h_{u,k} \in R^{\frac{D}{K}}$ is the projected feature in latent topic-aware subspace. It introduces topic prior guidance module as regularizer which leverages topic modeling to obtain global statistical knowledge from textual content to encourage the inferential topic-aware subspaces to be more orthogonal. In its intermetapath mergence step, It uses multi-facet attention mechanism combine various metapaths, ensuring the retention of both structural and topic-related semantics.

Although GNNs have recently shown superior performance on many graph analysis problems than traditional methods. However, GNN explanation for link prediction is lacking in majority of literatures, and existing GNN explanation methods only address node/graph-level tasks which don't generalize well to link prediction tasks. Recently, researchers pay attention to studying GNN explanations for link prediction on heterogeneous graphs in aspects of connection interpret-ability and heterogeneity. Most methods generate explanations by searching subgraphs [24]. Generally speaking, a relation subgraph G_r is a subgraph of G which consists of all node-relation triples with relation r. Zhao et al. propose HGSL [6] which introduces a novel framework which is proposed for jointly performing heterogeneous graph structure learning, for each relation subgraph and GNN parameter learning which can deal with both heterogeneity and noise. HGSL generates subgraphs of each relation separately and each generated relation subgraph consists of the feature similarity graph, the feature propagation graph and semantic graph. In the feature similarity graph, it makes heterogeneous feature projection and metric learning to capture the latent relationships arising from node features. Specifically, it uses a K-head weighted cosine similarity function is given by:

$$\Gamma_r^{FS}\left(\mathbf{f}_i', \mathbf{f}_j'\right) = \frac{1}{K} \sum_k^K \cos\left(\mathbf{w}_{k,r}^{FS} \odot \mathbf{f}_i', \mathbf{w}_{k,r}^{FS} \odot \mathbf{f}_j'\right), \tag{3}$$

where $W_r^{FS} = \left[w_{k,r}^{FS}\right]$ weights the importance of different dimensions of the feature vectors. In the feature propagation graph, one feature similarity graph and two feature propagation graphs are generated and fused by a channel attention layer. Then, HGSL utilizes MP2Vec [25] for the set of metapaths to generate semantic graphs. These graphs are fused with channel attention layer to a learned heterogeneous graph and optimized jointly with two-layer GNN in classification tasks. As paths have smaller search spaces than general subgraphs making explanations more straightforward and accurate. In DisenHAN [15] which aimmed to achieve automatic path selection, given a target node, the model identifies the major aspect of the relation between node pairs and projects their properties into different subspaces, and propagate corresponding information semantically so as to automatically extract metapaths. For each meta-relationship group, the neighbor features under each subspace are aggregated to capture specific semantic information. Finally, the different meta-relationship information is combined. Though mining such rich structural semantics is able to reflect heterogeneous information, exploiting the unstructured text content of nodes can significantly improve performance of models, which suggests us to identify the hidden multi-facet topic-aware factors. PaGE-Link [5] first utilizes k-core pruning [26] to find paths and then performs heterogeneous path-enforcing mask learning which uses mask learning to select the explanation edges to form paths connecting source to target according to the values of two scores function which are formulated as:

$$\text{Score}(p) = \log \prod_{\substack{e \in p \\ e=(u,v)}} \frac{P(e)}{D_v} = \sum_{\substack{e \in p \\ e=(u,v)}} \text{Score}(e)$$

$$\text{Score}(e) = \log \sigma\left(\mathcal{M}_e^{\tau(e)}\right) - \log\left(D_v\right), \tag{4}$$

where $P(e) = \sigma\left(\mathcal{M}_e^{\tau(e)}\right)$, Score$(e)$ and Score(p) respectively express informative and concise of paths, Score(p) is implemented using Dijkstra's shortest path algorithm [27]. It handles heterogeneity by providing higher weights for more important edges, which both handles model transparency and graph heterogeneity.

Hypergraph neural networks and hypergraph convolution networks build upon the foundation of GCNs and are specifically designed to handle hypergraphs that can capture high-order relationships. These models are designed to handle hypergraphs, which allow for more expressive representations of relationships compared to traditional graphs. By considering hyperedges and their interactions with nodes, hypergraph neural networks and hypergraph convolution networks can effectively capture and model higher-order dependencies and complex relationships in data. In Deep Hyper-Network Embedding (DHNE) [28], hyperedges in the hyperedges are indecomposable, where it is not necessary for any subset of nodes to form another complete hyperedge. DHNE then use GNN to learn representation vectors of hypernodes and hyperedges. However, those models for hyperedge prediction above consider the collective behavior of all objects within the hyperedge, rather than considering pairwise relationships between individual nodes structure of networks. HeteHG-VAE [29] first maps a conventional heterogeneous information network to capture high-order relationships in heterogeneous networks, researchers propose extending the original HIN to a heterogeneous hypergraph. This hypergraph capture both the high-order semantics information and dependencies among nodes within the hypergraph. The proposed method consists of two encoder for heterogeneous node and hyperedge, respectively. These two components work together to project the nodes and their high-order relations into this shared latent space, the model can effectively capture the collective behavior and interactions among them. This allows for the capture of both the high-order semantics and complex relationships between nodes in the heterogeneous hypergraph, respectively denoted as $\widetilde{\mathbf{Z}}^{\mathcal{V}_k}$ and $\tilde{\mathbf{Z}}^{\mathcal{E}^{\mathcal{V}_k}}$

$$
\begin{aligned}
\widetilde{\mathbf{Z}}^{\mathcal{V}_k} &= f_{\mathcal{V}_k}\left(\mathbf{H}^{\mathcal{V}_k}\mathbf{X}^{\mathcal{E}}\mathbf{W}^{\mathcal{V}_k} + \mathbf{b}^{\mathcal{V}_k}\right), \\
\tilde{\mathbf{Z}}^{\mathcal{E}^{\mathcal{V}_k}} &= f_{\mathcal{E}^{\mathcal{V}_k}}\left(\mathbf{H}^{\mathcal{V}_k}\mathbf{X}^{\mathcal{V}_k}\mathbf{W}^{\mathcal{E}^{\mathcal{V}_k}} + \mathbf{b}^{\mathcal{E}^{\mathcal{V}_k}}\right),
\end{aligned}
\tag{5}
$$

where $f_{\mathcal{V}_k}\left(\cdot\right)$ and $f_{\mathcal{E}^{\mathcal{V}_k}}\left(\cdot\right)$ are non-linear activation function, $\mathbf{X}^{\mathcal{E}}$ and $\mathbf{X}^{\mathcal{V}_k}$ can be the initial F-dimension hyperedge features and node features, respectively. Different from traditional autoencoders which encourage perfect reconstruction by only penalizing the reconstruction error [30]. In HeteHG-VAE, we can accurately infer the stochastic distribution of the latent variables from the shared latent space by variational inference, which can reduce the influence of incompleteness and noise in networks. Moreover, To capture the importance of different types of nodes within each hyperedge, we introduce a hyperedge attention strategy. This module learns the importance weights of the nodes and incorporates them into the final hyperedge embedding. The model performs link prediction tasks by calculating the similarity between two node embeddings computed by:

$$
f_{sco}\left(\mathbf{Z}_i^{\mathcal{V}}, \mathbf{Z}_j^{\mathcal{E}}\right) = Sim\left(\mathbf{Z}_i^{\mathcal{V}}, \mathbf{Z}_j^{\mathcal{E}}\right),
\tag{6}
$$

where $Sim\left(\cdot\right)$ is a similarity measure function.

3.4   Methods Based on Adversarial Learning

Adversarial learning methods offer a promising strategy to deal with the complexities of link prediction in heterogeneous networks, which aims learning the underlying patterns and relationships in the heterogeneous network data. One common adversarial learning method used in heterogeneous network link prediction is the Generative Adversarial Network (GAN) method which typically consists of a generator and a discriminator. The generator can be used to generate virtual link data, while the discriminator can differentiating between genuine data and artificially generated data. The generator and discriminator learn against each other so that the generator can generate realistic data.

To address the issue of randomly selecting nodes in the network for negative sampling in heterogeneous network embeddings, HeGAN [31] proposes a solution that utilizes GANs to learn the distribution of nodes and generate improved negative samples. In this model, the generator is responsible for sampling latent nodes from a continuous distribution. By doing so, it avoids the limitations of random selection and enables more efficient and effective negative sampling. The discriminator collaborates with the generator to capture the complex semantic relationships within the graph embedding. This collaboration enhances the overall quality of the generated negative samples by incorporating the rich semantics of the network. In the real world, heterogeneous networks often have partially observed relations for various reasons, leading to sparse network data. To tackle this issue, MV-ACM [32] aims to capture graph structural information in each view of the network by characterizing each relation space from a singular perspective. The approach utilizes a multi-view architecture, where an adversarial learning process is employed to learn the complementary information among different relations. This allows the model to leverage the strengths of multiple views and enhance the overall understanding of the network. By integrating the different viewpoints and utilizing the adversarial learning process, MV-ACM addresses the problem of sparse network data in heterogeneous networks effectively.

To address this issue of not distinguishing between different characteristics and potential relationships of each attribute, model called MADRL for ADDI prediction [3] uses GAN to capture shared attribute representation and specific attribute representation. It first jointly selects representative drugs and discriminant features for each attribute with CUR matrix decomposition approximation method to find the most discriminative features. To find a left matrix $\mathbf{C}^m$ with the discriminative feature $\overline{C}_m$, the relative-error CUR decomposition for the original feature space of the mth attribute matrix $\mathbf{X}^m$ can be denoted as:

$$\| \mathbf{X}^m - \mathbf{C}^m \mathbf{U}^m \mathbf{R}^m \|_F^2 \leq (1 + \epsilon) \| \mathbf{X}^m - \mathbf{X}_k^m \|_F^2, \tag{7}$$

where $\mathbf{X}_k^m$ is the best rank-k approximation to matrix $\mathbf{X}^m$ and $\mathbf{U}^m \mathbf{R}^m$ is the coefficient matrix only related to its selected $\overline{N}$ drugs. It minimize Eq. (7) and uses an iterative algorithm by alternating direction method of multipliers.

To address the challenge called edge-type disturbance that existing methods in heterogeneous networks trained on verified edge samples from different types tend to learn specific information related to those types. When making predictions on unverified edge samples of uncertain types, the type-specific predictions can be contradictory. DRPM [33] contains a structural characterizer, a type differentiator, and a resilient predictor to resist this disturbance. The structural characterizer learns edge representations on different types. The type differentiator generates diverse type experts by distinguishing type-specific edge representations. These experts are then evaluated for their reliability weights using a resilient predictor. The predictor employs an iterative truth discovery approach to determine the weights of different type experts. TDAN [34] utilizes GAN to generate transferable type-shared knowledge to handle the challenge. MTTM [35] utilizes GAN, which comprises a generative predictor and a discriminative classifier. The generative predictor employs GCN to learn transferable feature representations that can effectively capture the underlying relationships and similarities between different link types. It aims to predict missing links in the network using these learned representations. The discriminative classifier, which contains two fully connected layers with an activation functions, attempts to distinguish between various link types. By leveraging this classifier, MTTM can effectively differentiate the different types of links present in the heterogeneous network. Through the combination of the generative predictor and the discriminative classifier, MTTM enables the transfer of knowledge among link types, facilitating more accurate predictions and gain a better comprehension of graph's underlying patterns and relationships. However, challenges such as training instability and hyper-parameter tuning persist in GAN based methods.

3.5 Methods Based on Collective Systems

Collective learning based methods leverage collaboration and information sharing among multiple learners (such as models, algorithms, or entities) to improve overall learning performance. This approach has potential advantages in processing complex tasks [36]. HPN [16] includes a semantic propagation mechanism that absorbs the local semantic of nodes with appropriate weights. It also incorporates a semantic fusion mechanism that learns the importance of meta-paths and combines them effectively. These mechanisms enable the capture of high-order semantics and complex relations among nodes in the network. HPN can alleviate semantic confusion which appears the growth of model depth and theoretically proves that these methods are essentially equivalent to multiple meta-paths based random walk. Most existing network embedding methods typically address heterogeneous relations in graphs but often utilize a single model for all relations without differentiation. In contrast, Relation and Heterogeneous Network Embedding (RHINE) [37] distinguishes between Affiliation Relations (ARs) and Interaction Relations (IRs), aiming to capture both the structural and semantic aspects of heterogeneous networks. For ARs, RHINE calculates the Euclidean distance as the measure of proximity between nodes. This approach facilitates the understanding of the underlying graph structure. In contrast, for IRs, RHINE models the relationship between nodes as translations. By treating interactions as spatial translations, it captures the semantic meaning embedded within these interactions. To incorporate both ARs and IRs, RHINE combines them by minimizing the sum of a margin-based loss function denoted as:

$$
\begin{aligned}
L &= L_{EuAR} + L_{TrIR} \\
&= \sum_{s \in R_{AR}} \sum_{\langle p,s,q \rangle \in P_{AR}} \sum_{\langle p',s,q' \rangle \in P'_{AR}} \max \left[0, \gamma + f(p,q) - f\left(p',q'\right) \right] \\
&\quad + \sum_{r \in R_{IR}} \sum_{\langle u,r,v \rangle \in P_{IR}} \sum_{\langle u',r,v' \rangle \in P'_{IR}} \max \left[0, \gamma + g(u,v) - g\left(u',v'\right) \right],
\end{aligned}
\tag{8}
$$

This loss function ensures that the embeddings generated maintain appropriate distances and relationships based on their respective proximity measures. A collective system is introduced by Ensemble Multi-Relational Graph Neural Networks (EMR) [38] which encodes graph structure information in relation graph into low-dimensional nodes and relationship embeddings by a feature mapping based methods and learning relation embeddings respectively, designs specific convolutions for each relation, and then aggregates the convolution results under all relationships. This EMR optimization objective is formalized as an ensemble message passing (EnMP) layer with multi-relations, which contains a feature fitting term and a ensemble multi-relational graph regularization term.

Multi-view representation learning has become a promising topic for capturing objects multi modal data, where related works can roughly divided into alignment representation and fusion representation. In alignment representation, the agreements form of each view are maximize by alignment to form a multi-view aligned space. Fusion representation aims to fuse independent features from multiple views into a compact representation. Li et al. [39] propose a generative and probabilistic model which integrates multiple perspectives (different angles or representations of the data) and multiple features (different attributes or representations of the data), using a generative approach to optimize the model's predictive performance. In existing fusion strategies, there is a limitation in capturing the interactions between different modes while encoding diverse attribute information into representations. To address this issue, Fusion of Heterogeneous Information for Network Embedding (FHIANE) [40] introduces a multimodal attributed network embedding algorithm comprising three main modules to extract features from multimodal information sources. Firstly, the structure module is designed to gain insights into graph structural properties. It enables the learning of specific representations for each modality within the heterogeneous graph. The second module is the heterogeneous graph convolution module, which focuses on learning modality-specific representations. By applying graph convolutional operations to each modality separately, this module captures the unique characteristics of individual modalities. Finally, FHIANE incorporates the modality fusion module, which utilizes an extended attention mechanism to merge the representations obtained considering multiple modalities.

3.6   Methods Based on Transfer Learning

In the situation where labels are often very scarce for new types and are expensive to acquire, existing methods face challenges due to limited number of samples. Transfer learning can be applied to solve the problem, whose main goal is to transfer knowledge learned from one domain to another related domain to improve the capacity of the model to generalize and its overall performance. In heterogeneous network link prediction, transfer learning methods include auto-encoder structure [41], self-supervised learning [20], meta-learning [42], etc.

A Dependence Guided Discriminative Feature Selection (DGDFS) [8] for predicting adverse drug interactions is proposed. The model first uses a dependency-guided method to select the most relevant features, and then uses a discriminative

Table 2. Comparison table to illustrate the advantages, disadvantages of link prediction techniques.

Category		Advantages	Disadvantages
Unsupervised learning	neighborhood with weighted	tackle unlabeled information	lack flexibility and accuracy
Machine learning	matrix factorization	suitable for large graphs	computational complexity
Graph neural networks	metapath based	capture semantic level information	depend on metapaths
	with random walk	consider heterogeneous contents data	not consider interaction between different attribute information
	others	corporate node and semantic level information	computational complexity and dependency on label quality
Adversarial learning	negative sampling strategy	extract high-quality negative samples	exhibit instability during training
	multi-view architecture	learn information between various relations	training complexity
Collective systems	collaborative approach	multiple layers of information	complexity in implementation
Transfer learning	self-unpervised learning	can train with few labeled information	not accurately represent underlying data and susceptible to noise

learning method to build a prediction model. With this approach, DGDFS is able to discover associations between multiple attributes and use these attributes to predict drug interactions. Ultimately, the model is able to effectively capture the interactions between different attributes and improve prediction performance. An inductive I-RGCN model [43] implements the drug discovery task as link prediction in the Drug Repurposing Knowledge Graph (DRKG) [44]. I-RGCN first puts the node features into the relational GCN (RGCN) [45], where the lth RGCN layer computes the nth node representation $h_n^{(l+1)}$ as:

$$
h_n^{(l+1)} := \sigma \left(\sum_{r=1}^{R} \sum_{n' \in N_n^r} h_{n'}^{(l)} \mathbf{W}_r^{(l)} \right),
\tag{9}
$$

where $\mathbf{W}_r^{(l)}$ is a learnable matrix and N_n^r is the neighborhood of node n under relation r. It then introduces a MLP to tackle the ultimate layer of RGCN model for all node pairs participating to a certain relation type in an inductive fashion. MLAN [42] realizes few-shot link prediction on heterogeneous graphs through meta-learning adaptive networks. It utilizes a multivariate attention mechanism to fuse different meta-paths while preserving structure and topic-aware semantics. By learning adaptive parameters, the model can quickly adapt to the new few-shot link prediction task. We present our taxonomy of medels on link prediction in heterogeneous networks, as shown in Table 2.

4   Application

Link prediction strategies in heterogeneous networks are important and fundamental problems that estimates the existence likelihood of a link between two nodes, which serves as the basis in many data mining tasks, such as recommendation systems [2], medicine interactions [3], etc. We provide examples of applications in various domains as follows.

4.1   Recommender Systems

Link prediction in heterogeneous networks for recommendation aim to predict potential or missing links between different entities in a heterogeneous network. In this context, the heterogeneous network consists of various types of nodes (e.g., users, items) and different types of relations (e.g., user-item interactions, item-item similarities etc.). For example, MEIRec [2] introduces a metapath-guided GNN based on hierarchical attention, which aims to provide search intent recommendation in heterogeneous networks. The model incorporates both node-level and semantic-level attentions. This allows the model to assign varying levels of significance to different paths based on their relevance to the search intent.

4.2   Medicine Interactions

There are many tasks to tackle in medicine interaction areas, such as drug-drug interaction (ADDI) [3], new drug discovery, etc. Due to the multiply attributes of drugs, researchers have increasingly turned to multiview or multi-modal learning in order to predict ADDIs. DGDFS [8] based on molecular structures and side effects of drugs estabilish heterogeneous graph for ADDI prediction. Ma et al. [41] introduce a transductive model to infer novel properties of drugs. MADRL [3] can explore the effects of different attributes on ADDI detection. For drug-target interactions (DTIs) which need to analyze different interaction types, MPM [46] exploiting knowledge diversity across different link types to predict DTIs.

5   Challenges and Opportunities

Despite advancements in link prediction methods for heterogeneous networks, challenges still persist due to the complex and intricate nature of graphs. In this section, we propose potential avenues for future research about few-shot learning, dynamicity, and computation related to heterogeneous network analysis.

5.1   Few-Shot

The most popular strategies for tackling analysis in heterogeneous networks are based on GNN. These methods typically require a large labeled dataset to train models that can generalize well to unseen examples. However, traditional link prediction methods on heterogeneous networks face a significant challenge in situations where acquiring enough labeled data for all classes is expensive or impractical. To address this issue, several strategies have been proposed based on few-shot learning. The goal of few-shot learning is to learn from a limited number of labeled examples or new link types with few certain relation types. However, the majority of current few-shot based methods assume homogeneous graphs, making it difficult to directly apply these methods to heterogeneous graphs. Recently, IRGCN utilizes an inductive strategy to implement the ADDIs tasks [8], which demonstrates that the transfer learning has advantages in handling few-shot learning for link prediction on heterogenenous. Further research should be conducted on few-shot learning in heterogeneous networks, where the potential benefits of transfer learning be leveraged.

5.2 Dynamicity

Graphs are naturally dynamic where node or edge inputs may change time by time, such as social networks. Compared to static graphs, dynamic heterogeneous networks offer a wealth of heterogeneous information represented through different types of nodes and edges. DHGAS [1], a dynamic heterogeneous graph representation learning model, employs a localization and parameterization search space based on a multistage differentiable search algorithm. This approach allows the model to consider multiple types of neighbors across different time stamps simultaneously. In DHGAS, an attention-based message-passing mechanism is employed to integrate the dynamic and heterogeneous information from neighborhoods. Another model for dynamic heterogeneous graph representation learning is THGAT [47]. Similar to DHGAS, THGAT also incorporates an attention mechanism. However, THGAT introduces the use of time encoding technique suitable for real-time networks to represent temporal information directly. Furthermore, THGAT proposes three node signature methods to encode the heterogeneous information of nodes. Methods based on few-shot learning would also have advantages of addressing emerging issues such as dynamicity because it can catching up with the rapid growth of pairs of nodes and newly emerging classes. More methods should be developed to handle dynamic networks.

5.3 Computation

As the general strategies for link prediction are discriminative learning based methods of which the majority are based on GNN. However, real-world networks are often large and complex, making it challenging to handle the extensive node information. To address this issue and improve model efficiency, alternative solutions need to be explored as the deep architectures designed for graphs typically require significant computational resources. Therefore, few-shot learning and transfer learning based methods which have recently become a hot topic need to be studied urgently in the research area. Emerging technologies such as machine learning advancements can also be applied.

6 Conclusions

In this article, we conduct a overview of link prediction methods on heterogeneous networks. We divide researches for link prediction in heterogeneous networks into six broad categories: methods based on unsupervised learning, methods based on machine learning, methods based on deep learning, methods based on collective systems, methods based on adversarial learning, methods based on transfer learning. Then we introduce several applications of link prediction on heterogeneous networks. Finally, We provide several challenges and future research directions, where we will explore more efficient strategies for link prediction on heterogeneous networks.

References

1. Zhang, Z., Zhang, Z., Wang, X., Qin, Y., Qin, Z., Zhu, W.: Dynamic heterogeneous graph attention neural architecture search. AAAI Press (2023)
2. Fan, S., Zhu, J., Han, X., Shi, C., Hu, L., Ma, B., Li, Y.: Metapath-guided heterogeneous graph neural network for intent recommendation. In: Proceedings of the 25th ACM SIGKDD International Conference on Knowledge Discovery & Data Mining, pp. 2478–2486 (2019)
3. Zhu, J., Liu, Y., Zhang, Y., Chen, Z., Wu, X.: Multi-attribute discriminative representation learning for prediction of adverse drug-drug interaction. IEEE Trans. Pattern Anal. Mach. Intell. **44**(12), 10129–10144 (2021)
4. Davis, D., Lichtenwalter, R., Chawla, N.V.: Multi-relational link prediction in heterogeneous information networks. In: 2011 International Conference on Advances in Social Networks Analysis and Mining, pp. 281–288. IEEE (2011)
5. Zhang, S., et al.: Page-link: path-based graph neural network explanation for heterogeneous link prediction. In: Proceedings of the ACM Web Conference 2023, pp. 3784–3793 (2023)
6. Zhao, J., Wang, X., Shi, C., Hu, B., Song, G., Ye, Y.: Heterogeneous graph structure learning for graph neural networks. In: Proceedings of the AAAI Conference on Artificial Intelligence, vol. 35, pp. 4697–4705 (2021)
7. Cao, Y., Zhao, X., Chen, D., Huang, H.: Multiplex heterogeneous network representation learning with unipath based global awareness neural network. Futur. Gener. Comput. Syst. **150**, 317–325 (2024)
8. Zhu, J., Liu, Y., Wen, C., Wu, X.: Dgdfs: dependence guided discriminative feature selection for predicting adverse drug-drug interaction. IEEE Trans. Knowl. Data Eng. **34**(1), 271–285 (2020)
9. Wang, H., Cui, Z., Liu, S., Ni, Q., Gong, Z.: Evaluating edge credibility in evolving noisy social networks. IEEE Trans. Knowl. Data Eng. **35**(11), 11342–11353 (2023)
10. Ji, H., Shi, C., Wang, B.: Attention based meta path fusion for heterogeneous information network embedding. In: PRICAI 2018: Trends in Artificial Intelligence: 15th Pacific Rim International Conference on Artificial Intelligence, Nanjing, China, August 28–31, 2018, Proceedings, Part I 15, pp. 348–360. Springer (2018)
11. Rigatti, S.J.: Random forest. J. Insur. Med. **47**(1), 31–39 (2017)
12. Breiman, L.: Bagging predictors. Mach. Learn. **24**, 123–140 (1996)
13. Chen, H., Yin, H., Wang, W., Wang, H., Nguyen, Q.V.H., Li, X.: Pme: projected metric embedding on heterogeneous networks for link prediction. In: Proceedings of the 24th ACM SIGKDD International Conference on Knowledge Discovery & Data Mining, pp. 1177–1186 (2018)
14. Shi, Y., Zhu, Q., Guo, F., Zhang, C., Han, J.: Easing embedding learning by comprehensive transcription of heterogeneous information networks. In: Proceedings of the 24th ACM SIGKDD International Conference on Knowledge Discovery & Data Mining, pp. 2190–2199 (2018)
15. Wang, Y., Tang, S., Lei, Y., Song, W., Wang, S., Zhang, M.: Disenhan: disentangled heterogeneous graph attention network for recommendation. In: Proceedings of the 29th ACM International Conference on Information & Knowledge Management (2020)
16. Ji, H., Wang, X., Shi, C., Wang, B., Philip, S.Y.: Heterogeneous graph propagation network. IEEE Trans. Knowl. Data Eng. **35**(1), 521–532 (2021)
17. Zhang, C., Song, D., Huang, C., Swami, A., Chawla, N.V.: Heterogeneous graph neural network. In: Proceedings of the 25th ACM SIGKDD International Conference on Knowledge Discovery & Data Mining, pp. 793–803 (2019)

18. Cao, X., Zheng, Y., Shi, C., Li, J., Wu, B.: Meta-path-based link prediction in schema-rich heterogeneous information network. Int. J. Data Sci. Anal. **3**(4), 285–296 (2017). https://doi.org/10.1007/s41060-017-0046-1

19. Zhu, G., Zhu, Z., Chen, H., Yuan, C., Huang, Y.: Hagnn: Hybrid aggregation for heterogeneous graph neural networks. arXiv preprint arXiv:2307.01636 (2023)

20. Hu, Z., Dong, Y., Wang, K., Sun, Y.: Heterogeneous graph transformer. Proceedings of the Web Conference 2020, pp. 2704–2710 (2020)

21. Fu, X., Zhang, J., Meng, Z., King, I.: Magnn: Metapath aggregated graph neural network for heterogeneous graph embedding. In: Proceedings of the Web Conference 2020, pp. 2331–2341 (2020)

22. Veličković, P., Cucurull, G., Casanova, A., Romero, A., Lio, P., Bengio, Y.: Graph attention networks. arXiv preprint arXiv:1710.10903 (2017)

23. Xu, S., et al.: Topic-aware heterogeneous graph neural network for link prediction. In: Proceedings of the 30th ACM International Conference on Information & Knowledge Management, pp. 2261–2270 (2021)

24. Yin, Y., Ji, L.X., Zhang, J.P., Pei, Y.L.: Dhne: network representation learning method for dynamic heterogeneous networks. IEEE Access **7**, 134782–134792 (2019)

25. Dong, Y., Chawla, N.V., Swami, A.: metapath2vec: Scalable representation learning for heterogeneous networks. In: Proceedings of the 23rd ACM SIGKDD International Conference on Knowledge Discovery & Data Mining, pp. 135–144 (2017)

26. Bollobás, B.: The evolution of sparse graphs, graph theory and combinatorics (cambridge, 1983) (1984)

27. Dijkstra, E.W.: A note on two problems in connexion with graphs. In: Edsger Wybe Dijkstra: His Life, Work, and Legacy, pp. 287–290 (2022)

28. Tu, K., Cui, P., Wang, X., Wang, F., Zhu, W.: Structural deep embedding for hyper-networks. In: Proceedings of the AAAI Conference on Artificial Intelligence, vol. 32 (2018)

29. Fan, H., Zhang, F., Wei, Y., Li, Z., Zou, C., Gao, Y., Dai, Q.: Heterogeneous hypergraph variational autoencoder for link prediction. IEEE Trans. Pattern Anal. Mach. Intell. **44**(8), 4125–4138 (2021)

30. Probst, M., Rothlauf, F.: Harmless overfitting: using denoising autoencoders in estimation of distribution algorithms. J. Mach. Learn. Res. **21**(1), 2992–3022 (2020)

31. Hu, B., Fang, Y., Shi, C.: Adversarial learning on heterogeneous information networks. In: Proceedings of the 25th ACM SIGKDD International Conference on Knowledge Discovery & Data Mining, pp. 120–129 (2019)

32. Zhao, K., Bai, T., Wu, B., Wang, B., Zhang, Y., Yang, Y., Nie, J.Y.: Deep adversarial completion for sparse heterogeneous information network embedding. In: Proceedings of the Web Conference 2020, pp. 508–518 (2020)

33. Wang, H., Liu, R., Shi, C., Chen, J., Fang, L., Liu, S., Gong, Z.: Resisting the edge-type disturbance for link prediction in heterogeneous networks. ACM Trans. Knowl. Discov. Data (2023)

34. Wang, H., Liu, G., Hu, P.: Tdan: Transferable domain adversarial network for link prediction in heterogeneous social networks. ACM Trans. Knowl. Discov. Data **18**(1), September 2023

35. Wang, H., Cui, Z., Liu, R., Fang, L., Sha, Y.: A multi-type transferable method for missing link prediction in heterogeneous social networks. IEEE Trans. Knowl. Data Eng. (2023)

36. Xu, J., Han, J., Nie, F.: Multi-view feature learning with discriminative regularization. IJCA **I**, 3161–3167 (2017)

37. Lu, Y., Shi, C., Hu, L., Liu, Z.: Relation structure-aware heterogeneous information network embedding. In: Proceedings of the AAAI Conference on Artificial Intelligence, vol. 33, pp. 4456–4463 (2019)
38. Wang, Y., et al.: Ensemble multi-relational graph neural networks. arXiv preprint arXiv:2205.12076 (2022)
39. Li, J., Zhang, B., Lu, G., Zhang, D.: Generative multi-view and multi-feature learning for classification. Inf. Fusion **45**, 215–226 (2019)
40. Jieyi, Y., Feng, Z., Yihong, D., Jiangbo, Q.: Fusing heterogeneous information for multi-modal attributed network embedding. Appl. Intell., pp. 1–20 (2023)
41. Ma, T., Xiao, C., Zhou, J., Wang, F.: Drug similarity integration through attentive multi-view graph auto-encoders. arXiv preprint arXiv:1804.10850 (2018)
42. Wang, H., Mi, J., Guo, X., Hu, P.: Meta-learning adaptation network for few-shot link prediction in heterogeneous social networks. Inf. Process. Manage. **60**(5), 103418 (2023)
43. Ioannidis, V.N., Zheng, D., Karypis, G.: Few-shot link prediction via graph neural networks for covid-19 drug-repurposing. arXiv preprint arXiv:2007.10261 (2020)
44. Ioannidis, V.N., et al.: Drkg-drug repurposing knowledge graph for covid-19. arXiv preprint arXiv:2010.09600 (2020)
45. Schlichtkrull, M., Kipf, T.N., Bloem, P., van den Berg, R., Titov, I., Welling, M.: Modeling Relational Data with Graph Convolutional Networks. In: Gangemi, A., Navigli, R., Vidal, M.-E., Hitzler, P., Troncy, R., Hollink, L., Tordai, A., Alam, M. (eds.) ESWC 2018. LNCS, vol. 10843, pp. 593–607. Springer, Cham (2018). https://doi.org/10.1007/978-3-319-93417-4_38
46. Wang, H., Liu, R., Wang, B., Hong, Y., Cui, Z., Ni, Q.: Multitype perception method for drug-target interaction prediction. IEEE/ACM Trans. Comput. Biol. Bioinf. **20**(6), 3489–3498 (2023)
47. Zhang, L., Guo, J., Bai, Q., Song, C.: Dynamic heterogeneous graph representation learning with neighborhood type modeling. Neurocomputing **533**, 46–60 (2023)

Research on Firefly Algorithm Enhancement by Diversifying Swarm

Xiuqin Pan[✉] and Shuangqing Ren

School of Information Engineering, Minzu University of China, Beijing 100081, China
amycun@163.com

Abstract. In response to the issues faced by the traditional Firefly Algorithm (FA), particularly its tendency to become trapped in local optima and slow convergence during the global optimization process, especially for high-dimensional optimization problems, an improved version of the algorithm is proposed—Diverse Swarm Firefly Algorithm (DSFA). Enhancements to the algorithm are twofold: firstly, a new adaptive randomization parameter strategy is designed to meet the search requirements at different stages; secondly, a novel random search mechanism is introduced to enhance the diversity and quality of solutions during the iterative process. To validate the effectiveness of DSFA, simulation experiments were conducted on eight widely recognized benchmark test functions. The experimental results demonstrate that, compared to traditional intelligent optimization algorithms and another version of the improved Firefly Algorithm, DSFA exhibits significant advantages in both convergence speed and solution precision.

Keywords: firefly algorithm · population diversity · stochastic search · function optimization · convergence precision

1 Introduction

Amidst the backdrop of rapidly advancing technology, the significance of optimization problems has become increasingly prominent across various academic disciplines. Traditional algorithms often fall short when dealing with large-scale, nonlinear, and multimodal optimization issues that are prevalent in fields such as engineering, economics, and management. Intelligent optimization algorithms, which simulate the collective intelligence behaviors of groups, have demonstrated exceptional computational and searching capabilities, gradually emerging as an effective means to address these challenges [1, 2, 3].

The intelligent behaviors of biological communities in nature have inspired the innovation of intelligent optimization algorithms. These algorithms enhance the adaptability and robustness of the search process by simulating the interactions between biological individuals, thereby improving the efficiency of global searches. Among the myriad of intelligent optimization algorithms, Firefly Algorithm (FA) has quickly become a

This work was supported by National Natural Science Foundation of China (No. 62176273).

focal point of research in this field since its introduction by Yang in 2008 [4, 5]. FA simulates the bioluminescent and mutual attraction behaviors of fireflies, associating brightness with the value of the objective function, thus guiding the evolution of the algorithm toward the optimal solution. Despite its remarkable success in various applications, FA has also revealed certain limitations in practical use, including a propensity to become trapped in local optima, slow convergence rates, and low convergence precision [6, 7]. The existence of these issues restricts the broader application potential of FA. To address these challenges, researchers have proposed a variety of improvement strategies, such as incorporating chaos theory and adaptive parameter adjustments, to enhance the algorithm's global search capabilities and prevent premature convergence [8, 9].

This study conducted an in-depth analysis of the evolutionary mechanism of FA and proposed an improved Diverse Swarm Firefly Algorithm (DSFA), aimed at tackling the issues of being trapped in local optima and slow convergence rates during the global optimization process, especially when dealing with high-dimensional complex optimization problems. DSFA introduces adaptive parameter strategies and a search mechanism based on dimensional communication, enhancing the diversity of the population and the quality of solutions, effectively improving the algorithm's ability to escape local optima and its convergence speed. Through simulation experiments on a series of widely recognized benchmark test functions, the advantages of DSFA in terms of convergence speed and solution precision were demonstrated compared to other algorithms, thereby proving its potential and effectiveness in solving global optimization problems.

The rest of paper is organized as follows. FA and its recent progress are reviewed in Sect. 2. Our proposed DSFA is given in Sect. 3. Computational results on the benchmark set are presented in Sect. 4. Finally, conclusion is given in Sect. 5.

2 Related Works

2.1 Firefly Algorithm

2.1.1 Biological Principles

The bioluminescent phenomenon of fireflies, a natural mechanism for communication and courtship, serves as a fresh source of inspiration for algorithm design. Firefly Algorithm, drawing on this phenomenon, simulates the behaviors of mutual attraction and random movement among fireflies to develop an effective optimization technique. Fireflies communicate within their species through the light signals emitted by their bioluminescence, where the distinctive patterns of these signals are essential for intraspecific individual recognition. The flashing of fireflies not only attracts mates but may also act as a defensive mechanism to deter potential predators. As the distance from the light source increases, the intensity of these light signals decreases in accordance with the inverse square law and is influenced by atmospheric absorption, which restricts the range of their propagation.

The design of FA is based on three key behaviors observed in fireflies: the attraction between fireflies is not limited by gender, meaning any firefly can be attracted to the brightness of another; the attractiveness of a firefly is directly proportional to its brightness, with higher luminosity correlating to a stronger attraction; and as the distance between fireflies grows, both the light intensity and its attractiveness gradually diminish. These behaviors are mathematically modeled in the algorithm by establishing a positive correlation between light intensity and the objective function and by introducing an absorption coefficient to mimic the decay characteristic of light over distance.

2.1.2 Mathematical Model

In FA, the initial solution set is constituted by an initial population, where each firefly entity represents a candidate solution within the search domain. Assume that N is the population size, and X_i is the ith solution in the population, where $i = 1, 2,...,$N.

The light intensity (I) typically diminishes with an increase in distance. According to the literature [4], the light intensity can be defined as follows [4]:

$$I(r) = I_0 e^{-\gamma r^2} \tag{1}$$

where I_0 is the initial light intensity and γ represents the light absorption coefficient of the given transmission medium, which is commonly set to 1.0. The Euclidean distance r between any two fireflies, denoted as X_i and X_j, is calculated using the following formula [4]:

$$r_{ij} = ||X_i - X_j|| \\ = \sqrt{\sum_{d=1}^{D} (x_{id} - x_{jd})^2} \tag{2}$$

where x_{id} and x_{jd} are the dth component of X_i and X_i, respectively.

The attractiveness β is defined as follows [4]:

$$\beta = \beta_0 e^{-\gamma r^2} \tag{3}$$

where β_0 is a constant value and it is usually equal to 1.0.

When X_j is brighter (better) than X_i, X_i is attracted to X_j. It means that X_i will move to X_j because of the attraction [7]. The movement of fireflies is defined as follows [4]:

$$x_{id} = x_{id} + \beta \cdot (x_{jd} - x_{id}) + \\ \alpha \cdot (rand - 0.5) \tag{4}$$

where α is called randomization parameter and *rand* is a random value uniformly generated in the range [0,1] [7].

2.2 Relevant Improvements to FA

In recent years, FA has emerged as a research hotspot in the field of intelligent optimization algorithms due to its simple principles, minimal control parameters, high optimization accuracy, and ease of parallel computation. Researchers have proposed various variants of FA to address a range of benchmark and practical application issues. In this section, a concise literature review of this work is provided. These algorithmic enhancements can be broadly categorized into the following four types.

2.2.1 Enhancement of Firefly Encoding Methods

Throughout the development of intelligent optimization algorithms, Genetic Algorithms have stood as early paradigms, typically employing binary encoding for individual representation. Inspired by this encoding strategy, Supravo P et al. [10] introduced Binary Firefly Algorithm (BFA). This encoding method enhances the genetic diversity within the firefly population, thereby reinforcing the algorithm's diversity during the search process and effectively mitigating the phenomenon of premature convergence. In contrast, the basic Firefly Algorithm utilizes real-valued vectors for positional encoding, a simplification that, while reducing complexity, may lead to a deficiency in individual diversity during iterations, increasing the risk of becoming trapped in local optima. Zhang Jianfei et al. [11] proposed Quantum Firefly Algorithm (QFA) in 2014, which incorporates quantum information encoding technology into the traditional Firefly Algorithm to expand the search space and uses quantum rotation gates to update individual positions. This approach leverages principles of quantum mechanics to augment the algorithm's global search capability. Addressing the potential issue of premature convergence in the QFA optimization process, Zhao Junli [12] proposed a suite of improvement strategies. These include an adaptive step-size strategy to diminish oscillation phenomena around the optimal solution, a generalized elite reverse learning strategy to reduce the algorithm's dependency on the reasonable distribution of the initial population, and a boundary control strategy that enhances search diversity by increasing randomness in boundary individuals. Tao et al. [13] further introduced crossover and mutation operations from Genetic Algorithms into QFA, simulating crossover by exchanging quantum bits and mutation by altering individual quantum states. These operations facilitate the introduction of new information, thereby sustaining the diversity of the population.

2.2.2 Relevant Efforts in Amalgamating with Other Optimization Algorithms

In the domain of intelligent optimization algorithms, hybrid algorithms have increasingly become the focus of research. FA is renowned for its structural simplicity and intuitive operations, which facilitate the design of hybrid algorithms and aid researchers in constructing more efficient and robust optimization strategies. Li Yang [14] proposed an innovative hybrid Leapfrog Firefly Algorithm, drawing on the swarming strategy of the Leapfrog Algorithm to conduct localized in-depth optimization for each sub-swarm, achieving a more nuanced exploration of the problem space. Abdullah et al. [15] explored the potential of combining Differential Evolution with FA, introducing mutation operations from Differential Evolution to foster information exchange among fireflies and enhance the algorithm's search efficiency. Luthra et al. [16] proposed a hybrid Firefly Algorithm that integrates characteristics of Genetic Algorithms, enhancing population diversity through the incorporation of replication and crossover mechanisms, thereby aiding in the discovery of higher-quality solutions. Inspired by the solution update mechanism of the Artificial Bee Colony Algorithm, Pan et al. [7] proposed a novel search strategy to replace random movement, aiming to strengthen local search and provide more accurate solutions.

2.2.3 Research Endeavors Pertaining to Diverse Attraction Models

In the standard FA, the attraction between fireflies follows a full attraction model, where any firefly can attract any brighter fireflies [17]. However, this unrestricted attraction mechanism may lead to frequent changes in the direction of movement during the iteration process, causing oscillations in the search process and thus affecting the algorithm's convergence efficiency [17]. To address this issue, Wang et al. [18] proposed a neighborhood attraction model, which restricts the attraction to a local neighborhood, allowing fireflies to compare only with others within their vicinity. When the neighborhood encompasses the entire swarm, the model degenerates into the full attraction model. By adjusting the size of the neighborhood, an effective balance can be achieved between the algorithm's global search capability and local search accuracy, with the optimal size depending on the specific problem's characteristics. Pan et al. [7] also proposed an improved attraction model that adjusts the number of attractions between fireflies, reducing computational complexity and accelerating the convergence rate of the algorithm. Zhou et al. [19] introduced a partial attraction model, in which each firefly moves only towards a subset of better-performing fireflies. Verma et al. [20] proposed an opposition and dimension-based modified firefly algorithm, in which the movement of fireflies is restricted to moving towards the global best solution.

2.2.4 Adaptive Parameter Control Strategies

The performance of FA is significantly influenced by its control parameters, which have clear physical meanings. However, fixed parameter settings may lead to suboptimal performance during the optimization process, and adjustments are often required for different optimization problems to achieve better solutions, adding complexity to the application of the algorithm. To address this issue, Gandomi et al. [21] proposed an innovative FA based on chaotic mapping. This algorithm utilizes a chaotic mapping function to generate the light absorption coefficient and attractiveness values, thereby improving the algorithm's optimization capability. The introduction of chaotic sequences essentially traverses the parameter space, increasing the randomness of the algorithm and contributing to the diversity of the population, but it may also reduce search efficiency. The selection of the randomization parameter α is equally crucial for algorithm performance. An excessively large α may cause oscillations in the search process, making convergence difficult, while a too small α may lead to reduced search efficiency. To adapt to the search requirements at different stages, Yu et al. [22] proposed a strategy that dynamically determines the randomization parameter α based on the historical and current position information of each firefly. Wang et al. [23] further proposed a mechanism that dynamically updates the randomization parameter α based on the number of iterations. These adaptive parameter adjustment methods avoid the inconvenience of manually setting parameter values and further enhance the algorithm's optimization performance.

3 Algorithm Improvement

To address the limitations of FA, DSFA is proposed in this paper. Two revised strategies are incorporated into DSFA: (1) A novel adaptive strategy for the randomization
parameter α is designed, which dynamically adjusts the value of α based on the increase
in the number of fitness evaluations during the algorithm's execution. (2) A dimension
communication-based random search mechanism is utilized to escape local optima when
the algorithm's search becomes stagnant.

3.1 Adaptive Parameter Strategy

In the position update formula of FA, the randomization parameter α determines the
weight of the stochastic component within the algorithm, and this randomness can expand
the search range of the firefly population in the solution space, preventing premature
convergence. Reference [23] analyzes the convergence of the randomization parameter
α and proposes an adaptive parameter strategy as shown in Eq. (5):

$$\alpha(t+1) = \left(1 - \frac{t}{T_{max}}\right) \cdot \alpha(t) \tag{5}$$

However, its update strategy involves a linear reduction, which may cause the algorithm to be overly conservative in the early stages of the search and overly aggressive
in the later stages, making it difficult to balance the needs for exploration and exploita-
tion. Therefore, we propose a new adaptive parameter strategy, where the parameter α
is updated according to Eq. (6):

$$\alpha(count+1) = \left(1 - \frac{count}{maxFEs}\right)^2 \cdot \alpha(count) \tag{6}$$

where $count$ is the current number of fitness evaluations, $maxFEs$ is the maximum
number of fitness evaluations, and $\alpha(count)$ is the value of α at the $count$-th fitness
evaluation.

The strategy of parabolic reduction allows the algorithm to more aggressively explore
the solution space initially, transitioning gradually to a smoother and more refined search
as iterations progress. This helps the algorithm avoid premature convergence while
maintaining a degree of exploratory capacity in the later stages of the search. DSFA
uses the number of fitness evaluations as a quantitative indicator of search progress.
This adjustment mechanism, compared to traditional methods based on the number of
iterations, more accurately reflects the depth and breadth of the algorithm's search in the
solution space, enabling the algorithm to dynamically adjust its search strategy according
to the actual progress of the search.

3.2 New Search Strategy

In the standard FA, a firefly executes a random movement if its brightness is higher than
that of its comparison target. However, this purely random walk is not always beneficial

to the optimization process, as it may not guide the firefly towards regions of higher-quality solutions [7]. To overcome this limitation, A novel search strategy is introduced in this study to more effectively explore the solution space and discover fireflies with greater brightness.

If the brightness of X_j exceed that of X_i, according to the algorithm's principle of attraction, X_i is attracted to X_j, thus moving towards X_j. Conversely, if the brightness of X_i does not surpass that of X_j:

$$x_{id}^* = x_{id} + \varphi \cdot (x_{id} - x_{is}) \tag{7}$$

where x_{id} is the value of the firefly x_i in the d-th dimension; x_{is} is the value of x_i in the s-th dimension; s is a randomly selected dimension from the position of the firefly x_i, which is chosen anew with each update of the position; and φ is a random value uniformly generated in the range $[-1, 1]$.

Additionally, a greedy strategy is employed to ensure that only positions explored through random movement are retained if they are superior:

$$X_i = \begin{cases} X_i^*, \; iff \left(X_i^*\right) < f\left(X_i\right) \\ X_i, \; otherwise \end{cases} \tag{8}$$

Our proposed random search mechanism, inspired by the position update strategy in Artificial Bee Colony algorithm, involves randomly selecting a dimension at each iteration, using its value as a reference point to generate movement directions, and adjusting the firefly's position by multiplying by a random step size. This strategy establishes an indirect communication mechanism among different dimensions of the firefly, allowing changes in one dimension to guide the search direction of others, facilitating information exchange between dimensions and promoting coordinated search behavior in the multidimensional search space. This collaborative search mechanism not only avoids the limitations of independent searches in multidimensional space but also helps the population discover new, unexplored solutions by considering the interactions between different dimensions, thereby accelerating the convergence of the algorithm. The introduction of randomness at each iteration significantly increases the diversity of firefly positions within the population, a key factor in evolutionary algorithms to prevent premature convergence and ensure comprehensive exploration of the solution space. Through communication between dimensions, the algorithm can avoid getting trapped in "canyons" or "tunnels" in the fitness landscape, areas that may seem promising on a single dimension but are distant from the optimal solution from a global perspective. Finally, the greedy strategy, which updates the firefly's position only when the new position is better, further ensures the maintenance and increase of population diversity.

3.3 DSFA Algorithm Procedure

Based on the mentioned algorithm improvements, An enhanced FA named DSFA is proposed in this study. The pseudocode of the DSFA is shown in the table below:

Algorithm 1. DSFA Algorithm.

Objective function $f(x)$, $x = (x_1, \dots, x_d)^T$

Generate initial population of fireflies $x_i(i = 1,2,\dots,n)$

Light intensity I_i at x_i is determined by $f(x_i)$

Define light absorption coefficient r

while (*count<maxFEs*)

for $i = 1:n$ all n fireflies

  for $j = 1:i$ all n fireflies

    if $(I_j > I_i)$

      Move firefly i towards j in d-dimension

    else

      Identify a random dimension s and reference its value

      Compute direction vector as the difference from firefly i 's position to the reference
dimension

      Determine a random step size for exploration

      Update firefly i 's position along the direction vector by the step size

      Apply boundary constraints to ensure the new position is valid

      Evaluate the light of the new position and move to if an improvement is found

    end if

    Attractiveness varies with distance r via $exp[-\gamma r]$

    Evaluate new solutions and update light intensity

  end for j

end for i

Rank the fireflies and find the current best

end while

Postprocess results and visualization

---

4 Experimental Verification

4.1 Test Functions

To validate the effectiveness of DSFA, eight widely recognized benchmark functions [7] are employed in this paper to test the performance of the optimization algorithm. The mathematical definitions, search ranges, and global optimum values of these benchmark functions are presented in Table 1. All tests are conducted as minimization problems.

Table 1. Test functions used in the experiments

Functions	Search range	Min
$f_1(x) = \sum_{i=1}^{D} x_i^2$	[−100,100]	0
$f_2(x) = \sum_{i=1}^{D} (\sum_{j=1}^{i} x_j)^2$	[−100,100]	0
$f_3(x) = \sum_{i=1}^{D-1} [100(x_{i+1} - x_i^2)^2 + (x_i - 1)^2]$	[−30,30]	0
$f_4(x) = \sum_{i=1}^{D} (|x_i + 0.5|)^2$	[−100,100]	0
$f_5(x) = \sum_{i=1}^{D} ix_i^4 + rand[0,1)$	[−1.28,1.28]	0
$f_6(x) = \sum_{i=1}^{D} -x_i \sin(\sqrt{|x_i|})$	[-500,500]	-418.98*D
$f_7(x) = \sum_{i=1}^{D} [x_i^2 - 10\cos(2\pi x_i) + 10]$	[−5.12,5.12]	0
$f_8(x) =$ $-20 \cdot exp(-0.2 \cdot \sqrt{\frac{1}{D} \sum_{i=1}^{D} x_i^2}) - exp(\frac{1}{D} \sum_{i=1}^{D} \cos(2\pi x_i)) + 20 + e$	[−32,32]	0

4.2 Experimental Setup and Parameter Configuration

The experimental environment for this paper is configured with a CPU: AMD Ryzen 9 7945HX; RAM: 16.00 GB; operating system: Windows 11; and the software environment includes PyCharm 2020.3 and Python 3.12.2.

The efficacy of DSFA is substantiated in this section by utilizing the minima of the eight benchmark test functions in Table 1 as case studies. Through computer simulation, the performance of DSFA, as introduced in this study, is evaluated and compared with that of traditional intelligent optimization algorithms and other improved firefly algorithms. The algorithms compared include Artificial Bee Colony (ABC) [24] algorithm, the standard Firefly Algorithm (FA) [5], and the improved Firefly Algorithm (NEFA) [7]. According to literature [7], a population size of 20 individuals was used for all algorithms, with the dimensionality of the research problem set to 10 and 30, When D = 10, the maximum number of fitness evaluations maxFEs is set to 150,000; when D is increased to 30, the maxFEs is set to 500,000. The value range of the functions is set according to Table 1. The parameter configuration for DSFA is as follows: the initial randomization parameter $\alpha = 0.5$, the initial attractiveness $\beta_0 = 1$, and the light absorption coefficient $\gamma = 1 / U^2$ (where U is the length of the search range of the benchmark function), while the parameters for other algorithms are set according to the recommendations in the relevant literature to ensure the validity of the comparison, and the detailed parameter configuration is shown in Table 2.

4.3 Experimental Results and Analysis

To accurately verify the optimization effectiveness of the algorithms and mitigate the impact of random factors on error, the performance is evaluated in this experiment based on the average best fitness values obtained from 30 runs of each algorithm, and the results are compared with those in the literature [7]. The results are compiled in Tables 3 and 4, with the optimal performances highlighted in bold font.

Table 2. Parameter description

Algorithm	Parameter Configuration
ABC [24]	$N = 20, l_{limits} = N \cdot D$
FA [5]	$N = 20, \alpha = 0.5, \beta_0 = 1, \gamma = 1$
NEFA [7]	$M = 6, N = 20, \alpha_0 = 0.5, \beta_0 = 1, \gamma = 1/U^2$
DSFA	$N = 20, \alpha_0 = 0.5, \beta_0 = 1, \gamma = 1/U^2$

Table 3. Comparative Analysis of Performance Metrics for Various Algorithms on Test Functions (10 Dimensions)

FUNCTION	FA	ABC	NEFA	DSFA
F1	2.01E–02	2.52E–05	2.47E–160	**1.19E–247**
F2	5.66E–02	1.57E + 03	2.37E–36	**1.84E-237**
F3	7.39E + 00	3.91E + 01	2.83E + 00	**0.00E + 00**
F4	1.91E–02	9.01E–06	**0.00E + 00**	**0.00E + 00**
F5	9.93E–03	9.68E–02	1.47E–03	**7.26E–04**
F6	-2.36E + 03	-3.93E + 03	1.54E + 03	**-4.09E + 03**
F7	1.78E + 01	2.29E + 00	9.95E + 00	**0.00E + 00**
F8	5.36E + 00	7.31E–02	5.89E–16	**4.44E–16**

Table 4. Comparative Analysis of Performance Metrics for Various Algorithms on Test Functions (30 Dimensions))

FUNCTION	FA	ABC	NEFA	DSFA
F1	4.66E–01	2.73E–02	1.67E–92	**0.00E + 00**
F2	3.59E + 00	2.63E + 04	7.18E–12	**0.00E + 00**
F3	7.10E + 01	2.26E + 02	2.47E + 01	**0.00E + 00**
F4	4.63E–01	5.40E–02	**0.00E + 00**	**0.00E + 00**
F5	1.03E–01	1.02E + 00	5.30E-03	**5.78E-04**
F6	−3.26E + 03	−1.02E + 04	6.49E + 03	**-1.26E + 04**
F7	1.14E + 02	2.76E + 01	2.89E + 01	**0.00E + 00**
F8	1.20E + 00	1.92E + 00	4.14E–15	**0.00E + 00**

Tables 3 and 4 indicate that when the dimension D is 10 and 30, DSFA surpasses other comparative algorithms on all benchmark test functions F1 to F8, demonstrating exceptional performance in identifying optimal solutions. Taking function F7 as an example, which is a quintessential nonlinear multimodal problem due to the presence of multiple local minima and typically poses a significant challenge to optimization algorithms, DSFA successfully converges to the global minimum value of 0, whereas other algorithms fail to break free from the confines of local optima. In the optimization of function F4, both NEFA and DSFA achieve successful convergence, yielding results that outperform FA and ABC. For the remaining test functions, DSFA also shows superior performance compared to other comparative algorithms. This suggests that in comparison to FA, DSFA has achieved a notable enhancement in optimization effectiveness, especially when dealing with more complex high-dimensional test functions, where DSFA can attain better convergence outcomes.

To better contrast the convergence capabilities of DSFA with other algorithms, Figs. 1, 2 and 3 present the convergence curves for functions F1–F8 by FA, ABC, and DSFA for $D = 10$ and 30, respectively. It can be observed that DSFA converges much faster on all eight benchmark test functions compared to FA and ABC, and the precision of convergence is also significantly higher than that of the comparative algorithms. Most comparative algorithms tend to become trapped in local optima early in the search, whereas the improved strategies introduced by DSFA enable the algorithm to escape from local optimal regions and achieve optimal solutions with higher convergence precision. For instance, with function F6, DSFA is able to directly locate the minimum of the function early in the search, regardless of D being 10 or 30, whereas the other comparative algorithms fail to find the optimal solution even up to the maximum number of fitness evaluations. DSFA exhibits stronger search capabilities in solving high-dimensional space problems, which confirms the effectiveness of the proposed improved algorithm.

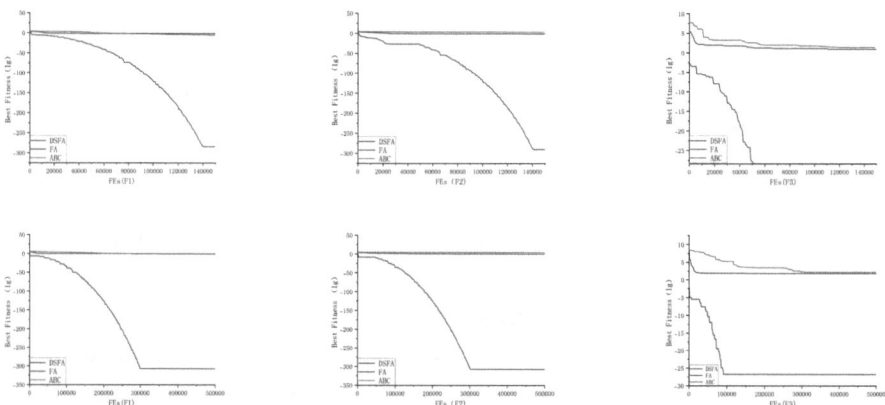

Fig. 1. Convergence curves for F1, F2, F3 ((10-dimensional above, 30-dimensional below)

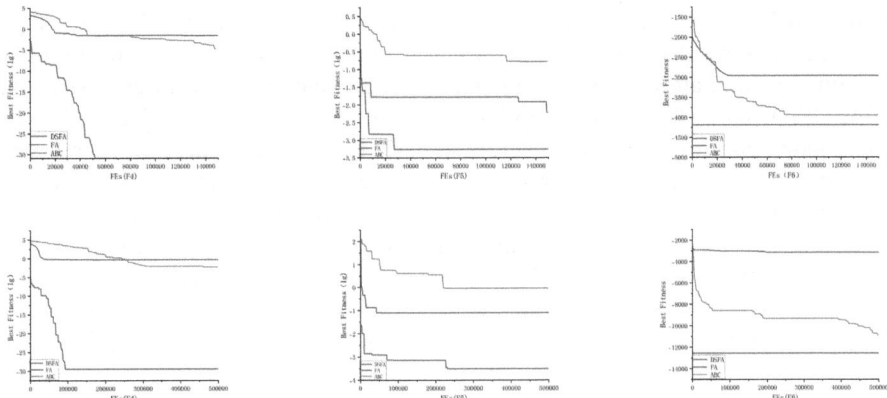

Fig. 2. Convergence curves for F4, F5, F6 (10-dimensional above, 30-dimensional below)

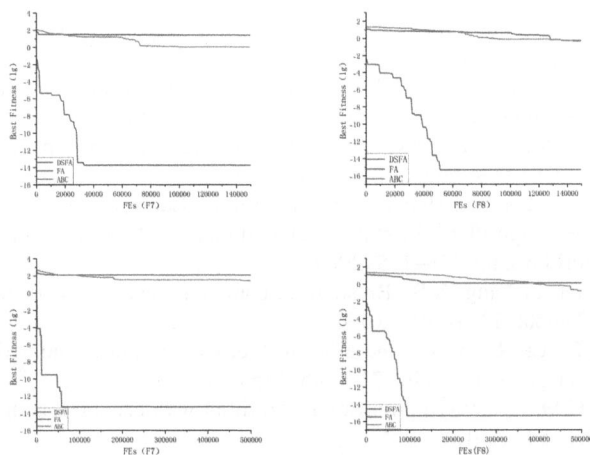

Fig. 3. Convergence curves for F7, F8 (10-dimensional above, 30-dimensional below)

5   Conclusions

FA is characterized by its simple structure, minimal control parameters, and robust optimization capabilities. However, it tends to exhibit premature convergence when solving high-dimensional optimization problems or when the search area is excessively large. To address these issues, Diverse Swarm Firefly Algorithm (DSFA) is proposed in this paper, enhancing performance through two main improvements. Firstly, the number of fitness evaluations is utilized as a quantitative measure of search progress, with the randomization parameter α being dynamically updated in a parabolic reduction manner, thereby eliminating the need for manual parameter setting. Secondly, a dimension communication-based random search strategy is applied to the attraction model, significantly increasing the diversity of the firefly population and preventing premature convergence of the algorithm. To validate the performance of DSFA, experiments are conducted using eight benchmark functions with different dimensions (10 and 30). Computer simulation results demonstrate that DSFA outperforms traditional swarm intelligence optimization algorithms such as ABC, FA, and the improved Firefly Algorithm NEFA. DSFA markedly enhances optimization performance and effectively addresses the premature convergence issue inherent in basic FA. However, the new search strategy proposed by DSFA only allows the value change of one dimension to guide the search direction of other dimensions, which may not sufficiently facilitate information sharing among different dimensions, and DSFA still has room for further improvement on certain function problems, possibly due to the presence of numerous local optima in such functions, which poses a certain degree of difficulty in the optimization process. Enhancing information sharing within FA will be the subject of more in-depth research in our future work.

References

1. Tian, D.P., Shi, Z.Z.: MPSO: modified particle swarm optimization and its applications. Swarm Evol. Comput. **41**, 49–68 (2018)
2. Yang, K., You, X.M., Liu, S., et al.: A novel ant colony optimization based on game for traveling salesman problem. Appl. Intell. **50**(12), 4529–4542 (2020)
3. Kohli, M., Arora, S.: Chaotic grey wolf optimization algorithm for constrained optimization problems. J. Comput. Des. Eng. **5**(4), 458–472 (2018)
4. Yang, X.S.: Nature-Inspired Metaheuristic Algorithms. Luniver Press, Beckington (2008)
5. Yang, X.S.: Firefly algorithms for multimodal optimization. In: International Symposium on Stochastic Algorithms, pp. 169–178 (2009)
6. Fister, J.I., Fister, I., Yang, X.S., Brest, J.: A comprehensive review of firefly algorithms. Swarm Evol. Comput. **13**, 34–46 (2013)
7. Pan, X., Xue, L., Li, R.: A new and efficient firefly algorithm for numerical optimization problems. Neural Comput. Applic. **31**, 1445–1453 (2019)
8. Liu, C.P., Ye, C.M.: A firefly optimization algorithm with chaotic search strategy. J. Syst. Eng. **22**(04), 538–543 (2013)
9. Wang, H., et al.: Firefly algorithm with adaptive control parameters. Soft. Comput. **21**(17), 5091–5102 (2017)
10. Supravo, P., Saptarshin, S., et al.: A cryptanalytic attack on the knapsack cryptosystem using binary firefly algorithm. In: International Conference on Computer Communication Technology (ICCCT), pp. 428–432 (2011)
11. Zhang, J.F., Du, X.X., Wang, B.: Adaptive enhancement of medical DR image based on quantum firefly and gain beta. Microelectron. Comput. **31**(5), 135–139 (2014)
12. Zhao, J.L.: Improvement of Quantum Firefly Algorithm and Its Application in Image Threshold Segmentation. Ningxia University, Yinchuan (2019)
13. Tao, S.B., Liu, D.Z., Tang, A.P., et al.: Bridge critical state search by using quantum genetic firefly algorithm. Shock. Vib. **2019**(2), 1–10 (2019)
14. Li, Y.: A Frog-Leap Firefly Algorithm and Its Application in Power System Scheduling with Wind Farms. East China University of Science and Technology (2013)
15. Abdullah, A., Deris, S., Mohamad, M.S., Hashim, S.Z.M.: A new hybrid firefly algorithm for complex and nonlinear problems. In: Distributed Computing and Artificial Intelligence, pp. 673–680 (2012)
16. Luthra, J., Pal, S.K.: A hybrid firefly algorithm using genetic operator for the cryptanalysis of a monoalphabetic substitution cipher. Inform. Commun. Technol. 202–207 (2011)

17. Wang, H., Wang, W.J., Sun, H., et al.: Firefly algorithm with random attraction. Int. J. Bio-Ins. Comput. **8**(1), 33–41 (2016)
18. Wang, H., Wang, W.J., Zhou, X.Y., et al.: Firefly algorithm with neighborhood attraction. Inf. Sci. **382**(383), 374–387 (2017)
19. Zhou, L., Ding, L., Ma, M., et al.: An accurate partially attracted firefly algorithm. Computing **101**(5), 477–493 (2019)
20. Verma, O.P., Aggarwal, D., Patodi, T.: Opposition and dimensional based modified firefly algorithm. Expert Syst. Appl. **44**, 168–176 (2016)
21. Gandomi, A.H., Yang, X., Talatahari, S.: Firefly algorithm with chaos. Commun. Nonlinear Sci. Numer. Simul. **18**, 89–98 (2013)
22. Yu, S.H., Yang, S.L., Su, S.B.: Self-adaptive step firefly algorithm. J. Appl. Math. **1**, 718–726 (2013)
23. Wang, H., Zhou, X.Y., Sun, H., et al.: Firefly algorithm with adaptive control parameters. Soft. Comput. **21**(17), 5091–5102 (2017)
24. Karaboga, D., Akay, B.: A comparative study of Artificial Bee Colony algorithm. Appl. Math. Comput. **214**(1), 108–132 (2009)

A Survey on Anomaly Detection with Few-Shot Learning

Junyang Chen[1], Changbo Wang[2], Yifan Hong[3], Rui Mi[3], Liang-Jie Zhang[1],
Yirui Wu[4], Huan Wang[3], and Yue Zhou[5(✉)]

[1] College of Computer Science and Software Engineering, Shenzhen University,
Shenzhen, China
`junyangchen@szu.edu.cn, zhanglj@ieee.org`
[2] Center of Health Administration and Development Studies, Hubei University of
Medicine, Shiyan, China
[3] College of Informatics, Huazhong Agricultural University, Wuhan, China
`{hongyifan,mirui2023}@webmail.hzau.edu.cn, hwang@mail.hzau.edu.cn`
[4] Hohai University, Nanjing, China
`wuyirui@hhu.edu.cn`
[5] Department of Obstetrics and Gynecology, Tianyou Hospital Affiliated to Wuhan
University of Science and Technology, Wuhan, China
`422753331@qq.com`

Abstract. The primary objective of anomaly detection is to identify abnormal or unusual patterns within a dataset, where the number of normal samples typically exceeds that of abnormal samples. Due to the scarcity of labeled abnormal samples, traditional methods face challenges when dealing with anomaly detection. To overcome these limitations, few-shot learning has emerged as a promising solution. By leveraging a limited number of labeled anomaly samples, few-shot learning enables the construction of models that enhance anomaly detection performance and generalization. This paper provides a comprehensive investigation of anomaly detection, covering its definition, fundamental principles, methods, and challenges. Furthermore, it introduces few-shot learning as a solution and explores its principles, applications, and technical categorization, including meta-learning, transfer learning, generative models, prototypical learning, and siamese networks. The paper explores the utilization of few-shot learning in anomaly detection across diverse data types This paper delves into significance across different domains. Additionally, it addresses the challenges faced by few-shot learning in the field of anomaly detection and proposes future directions for development. This comprehensive analysis aims to provide profound insights and guidance for prospective research and application in anomaly detection.

Keywords: Anomaly detection · Few-shot learning

© The Author(s), under exclusive license to Springer Nature Switzerland AG 2025
R. Xu et al. (Eds.): ICCC 2024, LNCS 15426, pp. 34–50, 2025.
https://doi.org/10.1007/978-3-031-77954-1_3

1 Introduction

In today's big data era, anomaly detection, as a key task in the field of data analysis, plays an important role in finding anomalies or abnormal behaviors that do not conform to normal patterns. The application of anomaly detection extends across various fields such as healthcare [1], industry [2], and cybersecurity [3]. The exploration of anomaly detection methods by researchers involves a meticulous examination of their effectiveness and applicability in different real-world scenarios. Researchers delve into the intricacies of algorithmic frameworks, statistical significance, and the optimization of anomaly detection models to address the evolving challenges posed by the ever-expanding landscape of big data.

In addition to traditional methods, deep learning has attracted lots of attention in anomaly detection [4]. Moreover, there are some review studies that explore in-depth specific application scenarios or technologies [5], which collectively shape the trajectory of anomaly detection research in a rigorous academic style. Collectively, these surveys provide insights into diverse anomaly detection approaches across various domains. However, existing anomaly detection methods face challenges in acquiring anomaly samples and generalization capabilities. To address these challenges, Few-shot learning methods have been proposed as a solution. Few-shot learning methods seek to enhance anomaly detection performance and generalization by utilizing a small number of labeled anomaly samples to construct a model. In this paper, we deeply review the common challenges faced by traditional methods and deep learning methods. At the same time, the principles and applications of FSL are explored in detail, including its technical classification. We also focus on the application of FSL in anomaly detection across various data types. Simultaneously, we comprehensively analyze the challenges faced by the anomaly detection field, providing valuable insights for future research directions and methodologies. Our contributions are summarized as follows:

- **The first survey in anomaly detection with few-shot learning.** To the best of our knowledge, our survey is the first to review the state-of-the-art anomaly detection methods with few-shot learning.
- **A systematic and comprehensive review.** By reviewing anomaly detection methods in various data types, The paper introduces the fundamental principles and methods of few-shot learning, along with its applications. A brief timeline of anomaly detection with few-shot learning is given in Fig. 1.
- **Challenges and future directions.** The paper offers valuable insights and guidance for future research in the field of anomaly detection with few-shot.

2 Anomaly Detection

In this section, we introduce a comprehensive definition of anomaly detection in various data types. The detailed descriptions of the notations used in this survey can be found in Table 1.

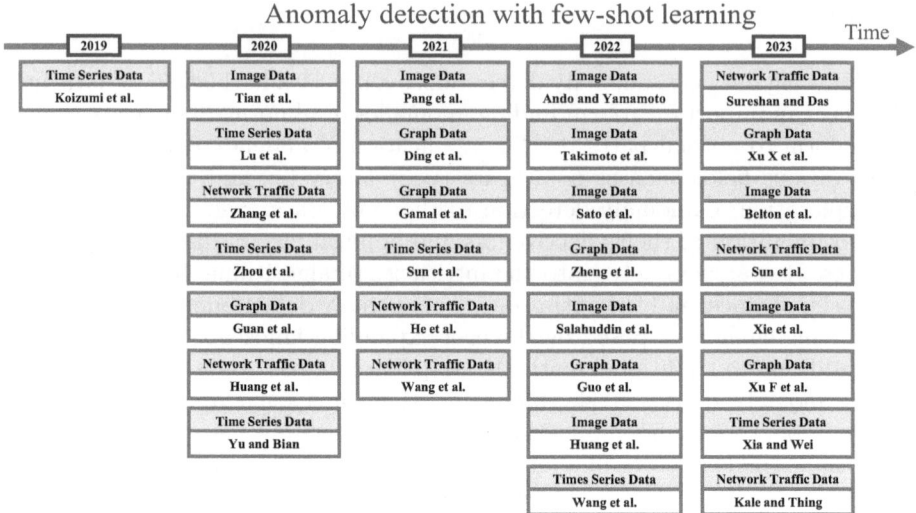

Fig. 1. A Timeline of Anomaly Detection with FSL.

2.1 Definition

Anomaly detection can be defined as follows: Given a dataset S consisting of n samples $S = \{s_1, s_2, \ldots, s_n\}$, the objective is to find a function $g(s)$ that can score or label each sample, indicating whether it belongs to the normal data distribution. In other words, the goal of anomaly detection is to identify a decision function such that for any sample $s \in S$, when the value of $g(s)$ exceeds a certain threshold, it is labeled as an anomaly. In this definition, the output of the function $g(s)$ can be considered as a measure of the anomaly level for the sample s, while the choice of the threshold determines when a sample is deemed anomalous. This definition provides flexibility to anomaly detection, allowing for the adjustment of the decision function's sensitivity based on specific scenarios and application requirements, thereby better adapting to different data distributions and anomaly patterns.

Time Series Anomaly Detection. Time series anomaly detection refers to the process of identifying data points or periods in time series data that are significantly different from normal patterns. Consider a time series $T = \{t_1, t_2, \ldots, t_n\}$ and the corresponding values $V = \{v_1, v_2, \ldots, v_n\}$. An anomaly in the time series can be defined as a deviation from the expected temporal pattern:

$$A(T) = \{t_i \mid |v_i - \hat{v}_i| > \delta\sigma_v\}. \tag{1}$$

Time series anomaly detection emphasizes the identification of abnormal patterns in time-ordered data, applicable in fields such as finance and production process monitoring. Typical anomalies involve unusual peaks, abnormal trends,

Table 1. Commonly Used Notations

Notation	Descriptions
S	A collection of n samples.
$g(\cdot)$	Function for assessing data normality
T	Time series
V	Time series corresponding values
t_i	Time point in the time series
v_i	Observation at time t_i
$\hat{v}_i$	Expected value at time t_i
σ_v	The standard deviation of the residuals
δ	Threshold for anomaly detection
I	Collection of image samples
X_i	Feature representation of the i-th image
y_i	Label of the i-th traffic sample
Y_i	Label of the i-th image sample

or patterns deviating from historical data in time series. Challenges in time series anomaly detection include sensitivity to temporal dependencies and trends, as well as the real-time processing requirements for long time series.

Network Traffic Anomaly Detection. Network Traffic Anomaly Detection aims to identify anomalous samples that deviate from normal network traffic behavior. We can define a binary label vector, denoted as $Y = [y_1, y_2, \dots, y_n]$, where $y_i \in \{0, 1\}$ represents whether sample x_i is an anomaly. When $y_i = 0$, it indicates that the sample represents normal traffic, while $y_i = 1$ indicates an abnormal traffic sample. The task of network traffic anomaly detection is to learn a classification model, denoted as $f(x)$, with the objective of mapping network traffic samples to their corresponding anomaly labels. By leveraging techniques such as statistical analysis, machine learning, and behavioral modeling, anomaly detection systems can effectively detect various types of anomalies, including malicious attacks, network failures, configuration errors, and abnormal traffic patterns. The timely detection of anomalies enables network administrators and security teams to take proactive measures to mitigate risks, safeguard network assets, and ensure optimal network performance. [6] proposes a new method integrating FSL techniques to address challenges such as data imbalance and unknown attack identification, which brings new ideas and potential solutions to the field of network traffic anomaly detection.

Image Anomaly Detection. Image anomaly detection is the process of identifying those images or areas of the image in the image data that are significantly different from the normal pattern. In image anomaly detection, we are concerned with unusual patterns, abnormal structures, or abnormal pixels in the image, which may be caused by errors, noise, fraud, or other abnormal conditions in the image. Consider a collection of image samples $I = (X_i, Y_i)$, where X_i represents the feature representation of the i-th image and Y_i is the label indicating whether the image is anomalous. The objective is to train a classifier capable of identifying normal and anomalous samples from given images. Image anomaly detection aims to identify abnormal patterns in image data, including unusual objects, abnormal colors, or textures. This field has a wide range of applications in computer vision and medical imaging. Challenges include sensitivity to image features and managing the complexity of processing large-scale image data.

Graph Anomaly Detection. Graph anomaly detection is a crucial research task focused on identifying and locating nodes, edges, or subgraphs that deviate from normal patterns within graph data. It involves the accurate detection of abnormal structures, behaviors, or attributes in the graph. In the domain of anomaly detection, four distinctive sub-fields are prominent, each addressing specific aspects of graph data: anomaly node detection, anomaly edge detection [7], anomaly subgraph detection, and anomaly temporal graph detection.

2.2   Review of Anomaly Detection Methods

Anomaly detection plays a crucial role in identifying unusual patterns or instances within a given dataset. This section provides a comprehensive review of various methods employed for anomaly detection, categorizing them into traditional methods, machine learning methods, and deep learning methods. The exploration of these approaches aims to offer insights into the evolution and diversity of techniques utilized in the field of anomaly detection.

Traditional Methods. Traditional anomaly detection methods can be classified into several categories based on their principles and technical characteristics. Such as density-based methods, statistical-based methods, measure-based methods. These traditional methods contribute significantly to the field of anomaly detection, offering various approaches and insights. However, they have limitations, such as sensitivity to data distribution assumptions, reliance on expert knowledge, and challenges in capturing complex patterns. Despite these limitations, traditional anomaly detection methods have played a crucial role in understanding and addressing anomaly detection problems. Anomaly detection across different domains has been explored several machine learning methods used in anomaly detection, including decomposition-based methods, Bayesian-based methods, Support Vector Machines (SVM), Isolation Forests (iForest), generalized linear models (GLM), clustering, etc. As advancements in this field persist, the synthesis of various techniques and the exploration of hybrid models may pave the way for even more robust anomaly detection systems.

Deep Learning Methods. Deep learning methods have become pivotal in anomaly detection across diverse domains. This review explores several key categories of deep learning techniques, including deep neural networks (DNNs), autoencoders, recurrent neural networks (RNNs), generative adversarial networks (GANs), and graph neural networks (GNNs).

DeepAD [8] highlights the efficacy of autoencoders. Challenges related to sensitivity to noisy data and hyperparameter tuning need attention [9]. RNNs, especially LSTM models, excel in modeling sequential data. GANs, known for generative capabilities, are applied to unsupervised anomaly detection. Models like MAD-GAN [10] showcase the potential of GANs in generating realistic samples for anomaly simulation. However, challenges such as training instability and hyper-parameter tuning persist [11]. GNNs, designed for graph-structured data, are widely used in anomaly detection in network data. Models like OCGNN [12], and StrGNN [13] showcase the versatility of GNNs in various graph-related tasks. They address challenges such as fraud detection and IoT network anomaly detection. Adversarial training, as seen in AEGIS [14], enhances model robustness in adversarial environments, providing a valuable tool for inductive anomaly detection. Contrastive learning, as demonstrated by SAD [15], leverages unlabeled samples for semi-supervised anomaly detection, showcasing its potential in anomaly detection tasks. Concerns about potential increases in training times arise with the introduction of additional learning processes.

2.3   Challenges in Anomaly Detection

Existing anomaly detection methods face challenges due to the rarity of anomaly samples, which complicates training models with sufficient accuracy. Methods must also adapt to new, unknown anomaly patterns, manage high data variability and complexity, and navigate issues in high-dimensional spaces like sparsity and the curse of dimensionality. Moreover, evaluating these methods is difficult due to the lack of anomaly samples, making it hard to choose suitable evaluation metrics and methods. To overcome these challenges, few-shot learning (FSL) methods have been suggested to improve performance and generalization.

2.4   Few-Shot Learning as a Solution

In anomaly detection, FSL provides a solution to challenges related to obtaining labeled anomaly samples. Traditional methods rely on a substantial number of labeled samples, which can be impractical due to challenges or costs. FSL addresses this by enhancing anomaly detection performance and generalization with limited labeled anomaly samples. While FSL enhances anomaly detection, challenges remain, such as the effective use of limited labeled samples and thoughtful model design and training. Future research efforts should focus on refining the application of FSL methods and exploring effective strategies for utilizing limited labeled data to drive advancements.

3 Anomaly Detection with FSL

3.1 Principles

Anomaly detection with FSL refers to the application of FSL techniques to anomaly detection tasks. In anomaly detection, labeled samples of anomalies in the data are often scarce. By employing FSL, the underlying principle of the model acquires feature representation or knowledge that can be generalized from these limited labeled exceptions to unknown anomalies. Through learning this generalized feature representation, the model becomes more adaptive in capturing the common characteristics exhibited by abnormal samples.

3.2 Common FSL Methods for Anomaly Detection

In the field of anomaly detection with few-shot learning, a variety of strategies have emerged to solve the challenge of training models with a small number of labeled samples. This section explores the key methods.

Meta-learning. In the context of FSL, meta-learning enables the training of a meta-model that can quickly acquire knowledge from a small number of labeled samples for new tasks and demonstrate strong generalization capabilities. Popular meta-learning methods include Model-Agnostic Meta-Learning (MAML) and Repeated Training in Inner Loop (Reptile), which utilize gradient-based optimization algorithms. By leveraging the power of meta-learning, FSL methods in anomaly detection address the challenge of limited labeled data and enable the development of effective anomaly detection models with improved performance.

During the meta-training stage in [16], MAML operates in an inner loop and an outer loop. In the inner loop, MAML first computes the updated parameter vector ϕ_i for each class i using training data D_i^{tr} and then it evaluates the loss term on the validation data D_i^{vd} sampled from the same class using the updated model parameters ϕ_i. The evaluated loss for each class can be written as:

$$\mathcal{L}\left(\phi_i, \mathcal{D}_i^{vd}\right) = \mathcal{L}\left(\theta - \alpha\nabla_\theta\mathcal{L}\left(\theta, \mathcal{D}_i^{tr}\right), \mathcal{D}_i^{vd}\right), \tag{2}$$

where $\phi_i \leftarrow \theta - \alpha\nabla_\theta\mathcal{L}\left(\theta, \mathcal{D}_i^{tr}\right)$ is the updated model parameter for class i. For classification tasks on image or bearing anomaly detection, the loss term is typically the cross-entropy loss. In the outer loop, MAML aggregates the per-task post-update losses $\mathcal{L}\left(\phi_i, \mathcal{D}_i^{vd}\right)$ and performs a meta-gradient update on the original model parameter θ as:

$$\theta \leftarrow \theta - \beta\nabla_\theta \sum_{\text{class } i} \mathcal{L}\left(\phi_i, \mathcal{D}_i^{\text{vd}}\right), \tag{3}$$

where β is the learning rate of the outer loop. At meta-test time, MAML can compute new model parameters based on a few samples from unseen classes and uses the new model parameters to predict the label of a test sample from the same unseen class. In summary, the essential idea of MAML is trying to find parameters of a neural network that do not necessarily have the optimal performance for different classes of data provided at the meta-training stage but can quickly adapt to new (unseen) tasks.

[17] introduces an innovative few-shot scene-adaptive anomaly detection method designed for videos. Following MAML, they adapt to a task $\mathcal{T}_i$ by defining a loss function on the training set $\mathcal{D}_i^{tr}$ of this task and use one gradient update to change the parameters from θ to θ_i':

$$\theta_i' = \theta - \alpha \nabla_\theta \mathcal{L}_{\mathcal{T}_i}(f_\theta; \mathcal{D}_i^{tr}). \tag{4}$$

The updated parameters θ' are specifically adapted to the task $\mathcal{T}_i$. Measuring the performance on $\mathcal{D}_i^{val}$ involves evaluating θ' as:

$$\mathcal{L}_{\mathcal{T}_i}(f_{\theta'}; \mathcal{D}_i^{val}) = \sum_{(x_j, y_j) \in \mathcal{D}_i^{val}} L(f_{\theta'}(x_j), y_j). \tag{5}$$

Its advantages include enhanced adaptability to new domain data and improved performance with limited labeled samples. MAMF [18] also contains such advantages, which utilizes multitask framework consisting of a feature extractor, an anomaly simulator by generative adversarial models, an asynchronous learner to create metatasks, and a type detector. However, challenges may arise in terms of model complexity, interpretability, and the need for diverse meta-learning strategies, which could impact real-world applicability.

Transfer Learning. Transfer learning in FSL entails pretraining a model on a large-scale labeled dataset, and then applying its feature representation or knowledge to the specific FSL task. [19] consider a GDN model represented by a parameterized function f_θ with parameters θ. The optimization algorithm first adapts the initial model parameters θ to θ_i' for each learning task $\mathcal{T}_i$ independently. Specifically, the updated parameter θ_i' is computed using $\mathcal{L}_{\mathcal{T}_i}$. Formally, the parameter update with one gradient step can be expressed as:

$$\theta_i' = \theta - \alpha \nabla_\theta \mathcal{L}_{\mathcal{T}_i}(f_\theta), \tag{6}$$

where α controls the meta-learning rate. The model parameters are trained by optimizing for the best performance of f_θ with respect to θ across all learning tasks. More concretely, the meta-objective function is defined as follows:

$$min_\theta \sum_{i=1}^{P} \mathcal{L}_{\mathcal{J}_i}(f_{\theta_i'}) = min_\theta \sum^{P} \mathcal{L}_{\mathcal{J}_i}(f_{\theta - \alpha \nabla_\theta \mathcal{L}_{\mathcal{T}_i}(f_\theta)}). \tag{7}$$

By optimizing the objective of GDN, the updated model parameter can preserve the capability of detecting anomalies on each network. Since the meta-optimization is performed over parameters θ with the objective computed using the updated parameters (i.e., θ_i') for all tasks, correspondingly, the model parameters are optimized such that one or a small number of gradient steps on the target task can produce great effectiveness. Formally, they leverage stochastic gradient descent to update the model parameters θ across all tasks, such that the model parameters θ are updated as follows:

$$\theta \leftarrow \theta - \beta \nabla_\theta \sum_{i=1}^{P} \mathcal{L}_{\mathcal{T}_i}(f_{\theta_i'}), \tag{8}$$

where β is the meta step size. [20] proposes a method that leverages registration, a task that inherently generalizes across categories. During inference, test samples that are out of the normal distribution are considered anomalies.

Each test image in $\mathcal{T}_{test}$ is assigned an anomaly score to the patch at position (i, j) based on the Mahalanobis distance $\mathcal{M}(f_{ij})$, where:

$$\mathcal{M}(f_{ij}) = \sqrt{(f_{ij} - \mu_{ij})^T \Sigma_{ij}^{-1} (f_{ij} - \mu_{ij})}. \tag{9}$$

[21] introduces MetaGAD, a novel framework for few-shot graph anomaly detection. MetaGAD leverages meta-transfer learning to navigate the challenge of limited labeled anomalies, with iterative updates to both the anomaly detector and the relational anomaly normalization module. The anomaly detector parametersΘ are initially updated:

$$\Theta' = \Theta - \alpha \nabla_\Theta L_{train}(\Theta, \Phi), \tag{10}$$

where Θ' denotes the updated Θ after a one-step SGD and α is the corresponding learning rate. Then they update the RAN parameters Φ as follows.

$$\Phi' = \Phi - \beta \nabla_\Phi L_{train}(\Theta', \Phi). \tag{11}$$

The framework demonstrates a promising approach to few-shot graph anomaly detection, showing its potential in scarcity of labeled anomaly data.

Generative Models Generative models are a class of models capable of learning data generation process. [2] proposes a few-shot anomaly detection approach using deep generative models for grouped data in industrial applications. By introducing a variational distribution $q_\phi(z|x)$, the marginal log-likelihood of a sample x is lower-bounded by the evidence lower bound (ELBO) $-\mathcal{L}(x)$ as

$$\begin{aligned} \log p_\theta(x) &\geq -\mathcal{L}(x) \\ &:= -D_{KL}(q_\phi(z|x) \parallel p(z)) + \mathbb{E}_{q_\phi(z|x)}[\log p_\theta(x|z)]. \end{aligned} \tag{12}$$

Then, the parameters θ and φ are updated to maximize the ELBO. $q_\phi(z|x)$ and $p_\theta(x|z)$ are implemented as an encoder and a decoder of the AE. [22] presents a simple approach based on the multi-scale framework, ANEMONE-FS, to exploit the valuable fewshot anomalies at hand. They adopt an anonymized subgraph sampling mechanism to generate graph views for contrastive networks. Taking a target node v_i for example, they generate its surrounding contexts by sampling subgraphs centered at it with a fixed size K, denoted as $\mathcal{G}_p^{(i)} = (\mathbf{A}_p^{(i)}, \mathbf{X}_p^{(i)})$ and $\mathcal{G}_c^{(i)} = (\mathbf{A}_c^{(i)}, \mathbf{X}_c^{(i)})$ for patch-level and context-level contrastive networks.

Prototypical Learning. Prototypical learning is an example-based classification method by mapping samples to a prototype space and using the prototypes for classification. This method usually uses a small number of prototypes to represent different categories, and the classification is performed by calculating the distance between the sample and the prototype. [23] proposes a novel framework, SG-ADNet, to help address the limitations of the single foreground prototype-based ADNet. This involves evaluating anomaly scores S per query feature vector using a negative, scaled cosine similarity measured to the foreground prototype p for that episode by:

$$S(x, y) = -\alpha d(F^q(x, y), p). \tag{13}$$

Here, $d(x, y)$ represents the cosine similarity between F. By computing the cosine similarity between query feature vectors and the foreground prototype, this approach can better evaluate anomaly scores and improve performance.

[24] leverages Energy-Based Models (EBM) with Langevin Dynamics proposes to address the challenge of modeling the intractable abnormal distribution. As the Langevin Dynamics proceeds, synthesized abnormal samples $LD(\hat{q}_m^i)$ are inpainted along the direction of q_m^i. The following reconstruction loss is introduced:

$$\mathcal{L}_{\text{rec}} = \frac{1}{m} \sum_{m=1}^{M} \text{MSE}(LD(\hat{q}_m^i), q_m^i). \tag{14}$$

By inpainting synthesized abnormal samples along the "normal" direction and employing a reconstruction loss, the approach aims to improve anomaly detection. Additionally, the use of a meta-learning scheme allows for effective adaptation in few-shot scenarios, minimizing the need for much training data.

Siamese Networks. Siamese network is a kind of neural network architecture commonly used in FSL tasks. The siamese network consists of two identical subnetworks that share weights and parameters. It takes a pair of input samples, such as an image or feature vector, and generates an embedded representation for each sample. The goal of the siamese network is to learn the similarity measure between samples, i.e. similar sample embeddings are close together in space and dissimilar sample embeddings are far away. FewSOME [25] differs from the typical siamese network as it trains on only one class and the number of branches in the network is a hyper-parameter of the model. The L_{dist} component represents the siamese architecture of FewSOME.

$$L_{dist} = \sum_{k=1}^{K} (||f(r_i) - f(r_k)||). \tag{15}$$

FewSOME differs from the typical siamese network as it trains on only one class and the number of branches in the network is a hyper-parameter of the model. The hyper-parameter K is the number of data samples that are input into f in tandem with r_i. The term $||f(\cdot) - f(\cdot)||$ is the ED between two feature embeddings divided by $\sqrt{l}$ where l is the dimension of the 1D feature embeddings. The application of siamese Networks [6] in anomaly detection allows us to effectively train with limited anomaly samples and provide accurate predictions when faced with new anomaly samples.

4 Applications of Data Types

FSL has demonstrated remarkable effectiveness in the realm of anomaly detection across diverse data types. This section provides an overview of its applications specifically in the context of anomaly detection for various data types.

4.1 FSL in Time Series Anomaly Detection

FSL is advancing time series anomaly detection, addressing limited labeled data challenges. Recent methodologies showcase efficacy in identifying anomalies within time series data. [17] introduces an adaptive anomaly detection method for videos, excelling in dynamic, unseen scenes. [26] proves effective across diverse video domains using self-supervised training. In medical imaging, [1] tailors a few-shot anomaly detection for abnormal frames in colonoscopy videos. Their approaches, alongside [24], demonstrate effectiveness in modeling abnormal distributions, enabling quick updates during inference without task-specific training. These advancements enhance FSL in time series anomaly detection, improving models' capabilities in various applications.

4.2 FSL in Network Traffic Anomaly Detection

The field of network traffic anomaly detection is indeed an active area of research, and researchers are continuously working on developing techniques and algorithms to improve the detection performance, especially in scenarios with limited labeled data. By leveraging few-shot learning (FSL) techniques, network administrators and security analysts can enhance their ability to detect emerging network anomalies and effectively respond to potential threats, even when labeled training data is scarce.

In a research work, [27] proposes a few-shot anomaly detection model specifically designed for malicious traffic. Their approach combines convolutional neural networks (CNN) and autoencoders (AE) to perform supervised pretraining and deep-feature extraction. By incorporating these techniques, they aim to enhance the model's ability to detect anomalous patterns in network traffic associated with malicious activities. [6] proposes the FSL-based siamese capsule network for intrusion detection. Their approach addresses imbalanced training data and aims to enhance the detection of unknown attacks through a well-designed deep-learning network and an integrated unsupervised sub-type sampling scheme. By employing the siamese capsule network architecture, they aim to capture fine-grained features and improve the model's ability to distinguish between normal and anomalous traffic. Lastly, [28] proposes an enhanced few-shot weakly-supervised deep learning anomaly detection framework. Their approach incorporates various techniques such as data augmentation, representation learning, and ordinal regression. By leveraging these techniques, they can improve the model's ability to detect anomalies in network traffic with limited labeled data.

4.3   FSL in Image Anomaly Detection

FSL for anomaly detection in image data is a critical area of research in industrial settings. Various methods have been proposed to address the challenge of training anomaly detectors with limited labeled samples.

One approach focuses on incorporating learning from inliers to improve the sensitivity to outliers [29]. Another method utilizes weakly supervised learning to train discriminative detection models with limited labeled anomaly examples, providing explainability in anomaly detection [30].

Deep generative models have also been explored for few-shot anomaly detection in industrial applications, capturing the underlying distribution of normal data and detecting deviations as anomalies [2]. [23] incorporates multiple prototypes, while [20] focuses on leveraging image alignment. [25] presents a low-complexity deep one-class anomaly detection method, and [31] proposes a few-shot anomaly detection model tailored for industrial cyber-physical systems. Additionally, [32] introduces a novel model specifically designed for few-shot anomaly detection in industrial vision.

FSL for anomaly detection in image data is a critical area of research, particularly in industrial settings [29] where anomaly detection plays a vital role in maintaining system integrity and ensuring safety. Various methods have been proposed to tackle the challenge of training anomaly detectors with limited labeled samples. [1] proposes a few-shot anomaly detection method for polyp frames in colonoscopy images, addressing inappropriate sensitivity to outliers by incorporating learning from inliers. [30] proposes an explainable deep few-shot anomaly detection framework, utilizing weakly-supervised learning to train discriminative detection models with limited labeled anomaly examples. [33] introduces an anomaly detection approach through FSL on normality, addressing the challenge of embedding normal classes into individually close but mutually distant proximities. [34] proposes an anomaly detection method utilizing a siamese network with an attention mechanism, addressing the challenge of limited abnormal data for visual inspection in manufacturing.

4.4   FSL in Graph Anomaly Detection

FSL has been increasingly applied to the domain of graph anomaly detection, which involves identifying anomalous patterns or behaviors in graph-structured data. Graph anomaly detection is challenging due to the complex interdependencies and structural characteristics of graph data. [19] proposes Graph Deviation Networks(GDN), a family of graph neural networks addressing the scarcity of labeled anomalies by enforcing statistically significant deviations between abnormal and normal nodes.

[35] presents CNN-IDS, an intrusion detection system based on few-shot deep learning designed for edge networks in the IoT. This model leverages a filtered information gain-based method and a one-dimensional CNN algorithm to identify zero-day attacks from the edge of the network automatically. [36] introduces a learnable hyper-sphere meta-learning approach, effectively detecting anomalies with changing boundaries in unbalanced binary classification settings. [3] proposes RNFSL, a cost-effective framework utilizing relation networks for anomaly detection in security applications, showcasing computational efficiency and reduced data requirements. [21] presents MetaGAD, a novel framework that learns to meta-transfer knowledge between unlabeled and labeled nodes in graphs for effective anomaly detection. [37] introduces FMGAD, a few-shot message-enhanced contrastive-based graph anomaly detector, leveraging self-supervised contrastive learning and a Deep-GNN message-enhanced reconstruction module for improved graph anomaly detection. These developments collectively highlight the evolution and diversification of FSL methods in graph anomaly detection.

5   Application Across Fields

The widespread application of FSL in anomaly detection highlights its exceptional performance across various domains, including healthcare, industry, finance, and cybersecurity. In the healthcare sector, this approach [1] demonstrates efficient identification of rare diseases and medical anomalies [38], providing an effective means to enhance the precision diagnosis of uncommon cases. In industrial manufacturing [2], FSL anomaly detection can monitor equipment and process anomalies on production lines, enabling real-time detection of potential faults. In the realm of cybersecurity [3], FSL provides a robust tool for detecting novel network attacks, and learning features of new attacks from a limited number of attack samples for early discovery and response to network threats. These instances underscore the diverse applications of FSL in anomaly detection across various domains, providing flexible and efficient solutions to address challenges.

6   Challenges in Anomaly Detection with FSL

Due to the complexity of anomaly detection and graph data mining, adopting few-shot learning techniques for anomaly detection also faces several challenges from the technical side. These challenges associated with few-shot learning are summarized as follows.

- Lack of labeled anomaly samples: In FSL, labeled anomaly samples are usually very limited or even non-existent. This makes it difficult to train the model to accurately identify anomalies, as the model needs to learn the characteristics and patterns of anomalies in a limited sample of anomalies.

- Class imbalance: In anomaly detection tasks, there are usually many more normal samples than abnormal samples, resulting in a class imbalance problem in the data set. This makes training and performance evaluation of the model difficult because the model may tend to learn more about normal samples than it does to capture features of abnormal samples effectively.
- Model generalization ability: In FSL, the model needs to have strong generalization ability, and can learn universal abnormal patterns from a small number of samples. However, due to the limited number of samples, models may overfit or fail to capture the variability and complexity of anomalies well, resulting in inadequate generalization.
- Potential data noise: During anomaly detection tasks, there may be situations where there is noise or mislabeling in the data, which can negatively affect the training and performance of the model. If abnormal data is incorrectly labeled as normal data or normal data is incorrectly labeled as abnormal data, this can cause the model to learn the wrong pattern.
- Representation learning: In FSL, how to learn feature representation with distinction and robustness is a key problem. Due to the limited abnormal samples, the model needs to learn effective feature representations from scarce samples to accurately distinguish abnormal and normal samples.

7   Future Directions

Future directions in anomaly detection with FSL involve advancing meta-learning strategies, enhancing interpretability, exploring innovative collaborative approaches like federated learning, and developing models resilient to dynamic data environments [39,40]. These directions aim to enable more adaptable, efficient, and accurate anomaly detection systems, ensuring their applicability across diverse domains and evolving data scenarios [41–43].

- Deep Learning and Reinforcement Learning: The integration of deep learning and reinforcement learning techniques aims to enhance the model's ability to represent complex data and adaptability.
- The application potential of few-shot learning: Utilizing few-shot learning to improve the model's generalization, strengthening its adaptability to new domain data.
- Explainability and Uncertainty Modeling: Emphasizing the interpretability of model results and modeling uncertainty in anomaly detection to enhance the model's credibility and usability.
- Federated Learning: Collaboratively training anomaly detection models using federated learning while safeguarding data privacy, adapting to data distributions across multiple geographic locations or organizations.

In addressing these challenges and future directions, researchers will continually explore novel methods and technologies for anomaly detection to accommodate the evolving application scenarios and data environments.

8   Conclusion

In summary, this survey provides a comprehensive exploration of anomaly detection with FSL, covering diverse data types and application fields. The review provides a thorough analysis of anomaly detection methods, challenges, and applications, highlighting the crucial role of FSL in addressing the complexities of anomaly detection. Delving into the principles of FSL, including meta-learning, transfer learning, generative models, prototypical learning, and siamese networks, reveals their significant potential in enhancing anomaly detection across various domains. The practical applications of FSL in time series, network traffic, image, and graph anomaly detection underscore its versatility. Nonetheless, challenges persist, underscoring the ongoing need for research and development. Looking forward, future directions advocate for advancements in meta-learning strategies, interpretability, and collaborative approaches such as federated learning, aiming to create more adaptable and effective anomaly detection systems. In conclusion, the evolving landscape of anomaly detection with FSL presents promising avenues for innovation and continuous improvement in addressing anomalies across diverse data types and application domains.

References

1. Tian, Yu., Maicas, G., Pu, L.Z.C.T., Singh, R., Verjans, J.W., Carneiro, G.: Few-shot anomaly detection for polyp frames from colonoscopy. In: Martel, A.L., et al. (eds.) MICCAI 2020. LNCS, vol. 12266, pp. 274–284. Springer, Cham (2020). https://doi.org/10.1007/978-3-030-59725-2_27
2. Sato, K., Nakata, S., Matsubara, T., Uehara, K.: Few-shot anomaly detection using deep generative models for grouped data. IEICE Trans. Inf. Syst. **105**(2), 436–440 (2022)
3. Sureshan, S., Das, D.: Few-shot learning based anomaly detection in security applications. In: Proceedings of the 6th Joint International Conference on Data Science & Management of Data (10th ACM IKDD CODS and 28th COMAD), pp. 295–296 (2023)
4. Lindemann, B., Maschler, B., Sahlab, N., Weyrich, M.: A survey on anomaly detection for technical systems using lstm networks. Comput. Ind. **131**, 103498 (2021)
5. Thudumu, S., Branch, P., Jin, J., Singh, J.J.: A comprehensive survey of anomaly detection techniques for high dimensional big data. J. Big Data **7**(1), 1–30 (2020). https://doi.org/10.1186/s40537-020-00320-x
6. Wang, Z.M., Tian, J.Y., Qin, J., Fang, H., Chen, L.M.: A few-shot learning-based siamese capsule network for intrusion detection with imbalanced training data. Computational intelligence and neuroscience **2021** (2021)
7. Wang, H., Ni, Q., Wang, J., Li, H., Ni, F., Wang, H., Yan, L.: Existence identifications of unobserved paths in graph-based social networks. World Wide Web **24**, 157–173 (2021)
8. Zhu, D., Ma, Y., Liu, Y.: DeepAD: A Joint Embedding Approach for Anomaly Detection on Attributed Networks. In: Krzhizhanovskaya, V.V., Závodszky, G., Lees, M.H., Dongarra, J.J., Sloot, P.M.A., Brissos, S., Teixeira, J. (eds.) ICCS 2020. LNCS, vol. 12138, pp. 294–307. Springer, Cham (2020). https://doi.org/10.1007/978-3-030-50417-5_22

9. Li, Y., Huang, X., Li, J., Du, M., Zou, N.: Specae: spectral autoencoder for anomaly detection in attributed networks. In: Proceedings of the 28th ACM International Conference on Information and Knowledge Management, pp. 2233–2236 (2019)

10. Li, D., Chen, D., Jin, B., Shi, L., Goh, J., Ng, S.K.: Mad-gan: multivariate anomaly detection for time series data with generative adversarial networks. In: International Conference on Artificial Neural Networks, pp. 703–716. Springer (2019)

11. Schlegl, T., Seeböck, P., Waldstein, S.M., Schmidt-Erfurth, U., Langs, G.: Unsupervised anomaly detection with generative adversarial networks to guide marker discovery. In: Niethammer, M., Styner, M., Aylward, S., Zhu, H., Oguz, I., Yap, P.-T., Shen, D. (eds.) IPMI 2017. LNCS, vol. 10265, pp. 146–157. Springer, Cham (2017). https://doi.org/10.1007/978-3-319-59050-9_12

12. Wang, X., Jin, B., Du, Y., Cui, P., Tan, Y., Yang, Y.: One-class graph neural networks for anomaly detection in attributed networks. Neural Comput. Appl. **33**(18), 12073–12085 (2021). https://doi.org/10.1007/s00521-021-05924-9

13. Cai, L., Chen, Z., Luo, C., Gui, J., Ni, J., Li, D., Chen, H.: Structural temporal graph neural networks for anomaly detection in dynamic graphs. In: Proceedings of the 30th ACM International Conference on Information & Knowledge Management, pp. 3747–3756 (2021)

14. Ding, K., Li, J., Agarwal, N., Liu, H.: Inductive anomaly detection on attributed networks. In: Proceedings of the Twenty-Ninth International Conference on International Joint Conferences on Artificial Intelligence, pp. 1288–1294 (2021)

15. Tian, S., et al.: Sad: Semi-supervised anomaly detection on dynamic graphs. arXiv preprint arXiv:2305.13573 (2023)

16. Zhang, S., Ye, F., Wang, B., Habetler, T.G.: Few-shot bearing anomaly detection based on model-agnostic meta-learning. arXiv preprint arXiv:2007.12851 (2020)

17. Lu, Y., Yu, F., Reddy, M.K.K., Wang, Y.: Few-shot scene-adaptive anomaly detection. In: Vedaldi, A., Bischof, H., Brox, T., Frahm, J.-M. (eds.) ECCV 2020. LNCS, vol. 12350, pp. 125–141. Springer, Cham (2020). https://doi.org/10.1007/978-3-030-58558-7_8

18. Hong, Y., Shi, C., Chen, J., Wang, H., Wang, D.: Multitask asynchronous metalearning for few-shot anomalous node detection in dynamic networks. IEEE Trans. Comput. Soc. Syst., 1–12 (2024)

19. Ding, K., Zhou, Q., Tong, H., Liu, H.: Few-shot network anomaly detection via cross-network meta-learning. In: Proceedings of the Web Conference 2021, pp. 2448–2456 (2021)

20. Huang, C., Guan, H., Jiang, A., Zhang, Y., Spratling, M., Wang, Y.F.: Registration based few-shot anomaly detection. In: European Conference on Computer Vision, pp. 303–319. Springer (2022)

21. Xu, X., Ding, K., Chen, C., Shu, K.: Metagad: Learning to meta transfer for few-shot graph anomaly detection. arXiv preprint arXiv:2305.10668 (2023)

22. Zheng, Y., et al.: From unsupervised to few-shot graph anomaly detection: a multi-scale contrastive learning approach. arXiv preprint arXiv:2202.05525 (2022)

23. Salahuddin, S.A., Hansen, S., Gautam, S., Kampffmeyer, M.C., Jenssen, R.: A self-guided anomaly detection-inspired few-shot segmentation network. In: Colour and Visual Computing Symposium (2022)

24. Wang, Z., Zhou, Y., Wang, R., Lin, T.Y., Shah, A., Lim, S.N.: Few-shot fast-adaptive anomaly detection. Adv. Neural. Inf. Process. Syst. **35**, 4957–4970 (2022)

25. Belton, N., Hagos, M.T., Lawlor, A., Curran, K.M.: Fewsome: One-class few shot anomaly detection with siamese networks. In: Proceedings of the IEEE/CVF Conference on Computer Vision and Pattern Recognition, pp. 2977–2986 (2023)

26. Sun, G., Liu, Z., Wen, L., Shi, J., Xu, C.: Anomaly crossing: new horizons for video anomaly detection as cross-domain few-shot learning. arXiv preprint arXiv:2112.06320 (2021)

27. He, M., Wang, X., Zhou, J., Xi, Y., Jin, L., Wang, X.: Deep-feature-based autoencoder network for few-shot malicious traffic detection. Secur. Commun. Networks **2021**, 1–13 (2021)

28. Kale, R., Thing, V.L.: Few-shot weakly-supervised cybersecurity anomaly detection. Comput. Secur. **130**, 103194 (2023)

29. Zhou, X., Liang, W., Shimizu, S., Ma, J., Jin, Q.: Siamese neural network based few-shot learning for anomaly detection in industrial cyber-physical systems. IEEE Trans. Industr. Inf. **17**(8), 5790–5798 (2020)

30. Pang, G., Ding, C., Shen, C., Hengel, A.v.d.: Explainable deep few-shot anomaly detection with deviation networks. arXiv preprint arXiv:2108.00462 (2021)

31. Sun, H., Huang, Y., Han, L., Zhou, C.: Few-shot detection of anomalies in industrial cyber-physical system via prototypical network and contrastive learning. arXiv preprint arXiv:2302.10601 (2023)

32. Xie, G., Wang, J., Liu, J., Zheng, F., Jin, Y.: Pushing the limits of fewshot anomaly detection in industry vision: Graphcore. arXiv preprint arXiv:2301.12082 (2023)

33. Ando, S., Yamamoto, A.: Anomaly detection via few-shot learning on normality. In: Joint European Conference on Machine Learning and Knowledge Discovery in Databases, pp. 275–290. Springer (2022)

34. Takimoto, H., Seki, J., F. Situju, S., Kanagawa, A.: Anomaly detection using siamese network with attention mechanism for few-shot learning. Appl. Artif. Intell. **36**(1), 2094885 (2022)

35. Gamal, M., Abbas, H.M., Moustafa, N., Sitnikova, E., Sadek, R.A.: Few-shot learning for discovering anomalous behaviors in edge networks. Comput. Mater. Continua **69**(2) (2021)

36. Guo, Q., Zhao, X., Fang, Y., Yang, S., Lin, X., Ouyang, D.: Learning hypersphere for few-shot anomaly detection on attributed networks. In: Proceedings of the 31st ACM International Conference on Information & Knowledge Management, pp. 635–645 (2022)

37. Xu, F., Wang, N., Wen, X., Gao, M., Guo, C., Zhao, X.: Few-shot message-enhanced contrastive learning for graph anomaly detection. arXiv preprint arXiv:2311.10370 (2023)

38. Wang, H., Cui, Z., Yang, Y., Wang, B., Zhu, L., Zhang, W.: A network enhancement method to identify spurious drug-drug interactions. IEEE/ACM Trans. Comput. Biol. Bioinform., 1–13 (2024)

39. Wang, H., Qiao, C., Guo, X., Fang, L., Sha, Y., Gong, Z.: Identifying and evaluating anomalous structural change-based nodes in generalized dynamic social networks. ACM Trans. Web **15**(4) (June 2021)

40. Wang, H., Qiao, C.: A nodes' evolution diversity inspired method to detect anomalies in dynamic social networks. IEEE Trans. Knowl. Data Eng. **32**(10), 1868–1880 (2020)

41. Wang, H., Cui, Z., Liu, S., Ni, Q., Gong, Z.: Evaluating edge credibility in evolving noisy social networks. IEEE Trans. Knowl. Data Eng. **35**(11), 11342–11353 (2023)

42. Wang, H., Gao, Q., Li, H., Wang, H., Yan, L., Liu, G.: A structural evolution-based anomaly detection method for generalized evolving social networks. Comput. J. **65**(5) (12 2020) 1189–1199

43. Wang, H., Wu, J., Hu, W., Wu, X.: Detecting and assessing anomalous evolutionary behaviors of nodes in evolving social networks. ACM Trans. Knowl. Discov. Data **13**(1), January 2019

Electromyography-Based Intentional-Deception Behavior Analysis in an Interactive Social Context: Statistical Analysis and Machine Learning

Zizhao Dong[1,2], Jingting Li[2,3]([✉]), Su-Jing Wang[2,3], and Gongxiang Chen[1]([✉])

[1] School of Education and Psychology, University of Jinan, Jinan 250024, China
sep_chengx@ujn.edu.cn
[2] CAS Key Laboratory of Behavioral Science, Institute of Psychology,
Beijing 100101, China
[3] Department of Psychology, University of the Chinese Academy of Sciences,
Beijing 101408, China
lijt@psych.ac.cn

Abstract. Lying is a common social behavior, and accurate lie detection is crucial in areas such as national security. However, existing lie detection techniques have certain limitations. Therefore, more accurate and reliable tools and methods are needed to meet the practical needs of lie detection. In this context, this study discovered the potential value of electromyography (EMG) as a lie detection indicator. Specifically, this study used EMG for statistical analysis and machine learning recognition analysis of the lying process in an interactive scenario of active lying. Furthermore, we compared the performance of two traditional machine learning models and one deep learning model for lie detection based on EMG signals. In particular, time-dimensional and time-frequency-dimensional EMG features were used to mine and lie related features. Statistical results showed that compared to truth-telling, people tend to suppress their facial expressions when preparing to lie. Some facial muscle movements that were not be successfully suppressed after lying may be crucial for detecting lies. Besides the statistic analysis, the analysis results of machine learning also demonstrated demonstrate the potential of machine learning models for EMG-based intelligent lying process analysis, particularly the RUSBoosted tree. In addition, our experiment result also proved that focusing on specific facial muscles, such as Corrugator supercilii, could improve the accuracy and efficiency of intelligent algorithms. In summary, our research results provide more insights into the cognitive and facial muscle movement patterns involved in lying based on statistical analysis and machine learning.

Keywords: Facial electromyography · Intentional-deception behavior · Interactive social context · Machine learning · Micro-expression

© The Author(s), under exclusive license to Springer Nature Switzerland AG 2025
R. Xu et al. (Eds.): ICCC 2024, LNCS 15426, pp. 51–67, 2025.
https://doi.org/10.1007/978-3-031-77954-1_4

1 Introduction

Lying is a common social behavior in daily life, with people lying on average one or two times per day [7]. When someone is lying, he or she may experience emotions such as fear, guilt, and excitement, which can manifest in physical responses that we maybe can use as "clues" to detect lies [12,32]. Unfortunately, despite the prevalence of lying and the manifestation of lying clues, most people have a success rate of detecting lies below or equal to 50% (random level), according to the majority of published studies [3,5,10,19,21,22].

The accuracy of lie detection is critical in fields like criminal justice, clinical medicine, and national security, where experts often achieve 80% to 90% accuracy [4]. These experts are quicker in judgment, more attuned to non-verbal cues such as facial expressions, and more sensitive to subtle emotional changes [16,25,33]. In high-stakes situations, facial muscles may involuntarily reveal genuine emotions, such as through micro-expressions [11,20,26]. Micro-expressions have been suggested as indicators for detecting lies [23]. However, detecting lies through subtle facial changes at the visual level is challenging. To address this, our study introduces electromyography (EMG) as an objective indicator to measure facial expressions. EMG signals capture facial muscle movements, allowing for the quantification of both macro-expressions and micro-expressions [1]. This method enables more accurate analysis and identification of lies.

For humans, the EMG-based lie detection analysis involves simply mapping the changes in EMG signals on the temporal or frequency domain. Nevertheless, delving deeper into the correlation between facial muscle movements and deception requires more than just basic signal processing and observation of EMG signals. This is where machine learning techniques excel, as they are capable of extracting high-level features related to deception from a large number of data [2]. In other words, machine learning could uncover subtle patterns and relationships in the data that may not be apparent to human observers. This highlights the potential of machine learning in the field of facial EMG-based lie detection.

When observing facial expressions with human vision, only the movement of muscles and changes in expressions can be observed. In contrast, small muscle activities or physiological signals cannot be visually detected. Whether it is facial expressions or micro-expressions, these behaviors fundamentally involve the movement of facial muscles. Therefore, we hypothesize that EMG signals generated by muscle movements can be used to replace visual information for analysis, leading to the same conclusions as previous research. In general, this study aims to further explore the feasibility and effectiveness of using EMG signal analysis methods to identify deceptive behavior based on existing research and to expand our understanding of deceptive behavior.

Specifically, we design a face-to-face interactive experimental paradigm with high ecological validity so as to collect EMG-based lying data. First, we identify the movement patterns of facial muscles during lying through statistical analysis based on EMG signal. Then, our study demonstrates that the system combining

EMG and machine learning can achieve intelligent lie detection by mining the physiological signal features during lying. Moreover, we refine the region-wise study of facial muscles and the phase-wise study of the lying process with the help of EMG acquisition system. In sum, these findings have the potential to enhance the development of more precise expert systems for lie detection and deepen our comprehension of the physiological and emotional processes involved in deception.

2   Related Works

The study of lie detection using EMG is still an emerging field and there is not much relevant research. In this subsection, we focus on reviewing related works on feature extraction and machine learning based on EMG signals, providing technical support for the intelligent lie detection analysis in this article.

Regarding feature extraction, EMG signal analysis through time domain information is an intuitive approach. Lola C and Karkar et al. increased the validity of the EMG signal by using a bandpass filter and a noise detection algorithm [14]. Nihal Fatma et al. reduced the dimensionality of the EMG signal by using principal component analysis (PCA), which aided in the computation and storage of EMG signal [15]. Anastasia Shuster et al. extracted the EMG features in the zygomaticus major and corrugator supercilii regions and applied machine learning algorithms to identify lies [30]. In addition, the importance of EMG frequency domain information is gaining attention. For example, Zawawi et al. used spectrograms to characterise the EMG signal and their experimental results proved its feasibility [35].

Regarding the machine learning, determining whether someone is lying or not is a binary classification task. For one-dimensional EMG signals, it is common to use some traditional machine learning algorithms for classification. This is because machine learning can look for patterns in data to give data-driven probabilistic predictions, and these patterns improve the interpretability of machine learning algorithms. For the binary classification problem, linear support vector machine (SVM) is a simple and effective machine learning method. Even if the sample size is relatively small, SVM can achieve good results [31]. Fricke et al. used SVM and K-Nearest Neighbors (KNN) to classify the different activities represented by EMG signals, where SVM outperforms KNN [13]. Furthermore, the dataset of truth-telling and lying samples suffers from unbalanced data distribution. However, traditional machine learning methods tend to create suboptimal classification models when there are far more examples of one class in the training dataset than of the other classes. RUSBoost is a very simple and effective algorithm for unbalanced datasets. For example, the effectiveness of RUSBoost was validated using 15 datasets from different domains and achieved good results for all unbalanced data samples [29].

Compared to statistic-based machine learning methods, deep learning based on neural networks is well able to mine advanced features related to labels. Convolutional neural network (CNN) was applied to classify EMG signals and achieved recognition rates of up to 67.6%, indicating the promising research approach of using deep learning for EMG signals [13] . For spectrograms, deep learning is more adequate for learning features. Joshi et al., created spectrogram images of segmented sEMG signals by means of the short time Fourier transform [17]. Ozdemir et al. collected EMG signals from arm muscles and trained a residual network (ResNet) using spectrogram to recognize seven different gestures, achieving 99.59% accuracy [24]. In summary, it is feasible to apply spectrogram images of EMG signals to lie detection using deep learning models.

3   Method

3.1   Data Acquisition

This study used a face-to-face interaction interrogation paradigm to conduct the experiment [34]. The experiment involved 22 volunteers, with a mean age of 24.59 years (SD = 2.99). The participants were randomly paired into 11 groups, with each pair consisting of individuals who did not previously know each other.

In a face-to-face interrogation competition, participants were assigned the roles of interrogee and interrogator by alternating means. The interrogee was tasked with providing truth-telling or lying responses to the interrogator's yes-or-no queries regarding baseline information, autobiographical information, and personal preferences. For example, "Were you born in February?", "Have you ever seen the sea?", "Do you like coffee?" etc. Furthermore, the interrogator correctly recognized that the interrogee was lying in a trial, an additional 5 CNY bonus would be awarded to the interrogator. If the interrogator failed to recognize the interrogee lying in a trial, an additional 5 CNY bonus would be awarded to the interrogee. The bonus was set to stimulate strong competitive motivation among participants to deceive each other. The detailed process is shown in Fig. 1. The whole experiment was recorded.

Meanwhile, we recorded facial EMG at a sampling frequency of 1 KHz using EMG recording equipment and silver chloride cup electrodes. Regarding the electrode distribution on the face, we selected seven locations on the left side of the face for EMG signal acquisition, including frontalis (channel 1, C1), corrugator supercilii (channel 2, C2), orbicularis oculi (channel 3, C3), levator labii superioris alaeque nasi (channel 4, C4), zygomaticus (channel 5, C5), orbicularis oris (channel 6, C6), depressor anguli oris (channel 7, C7), as illustrated in Fig. 2. Specifically, the experiment was designed with electrodes attached to the left side of the face but not the right side. This asymmetric setup allowed the interrogator to observe changes in the expression of the participant's right face, while also capturing more pronounced facial muscle movements through electromyography, as studies have shown that the left facial region expresses emotions more strongly than the right facial region [9].

3.2   Data Annotation

As mentioned in Subsect. 3.1, we simultaneously recorded participants' audio signals during the experiment. This allowed us to segment and label the EMG

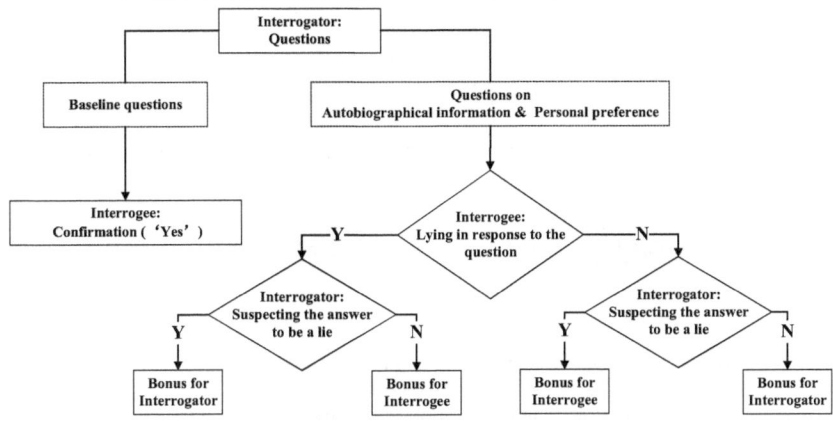

Fig. 1. Experimental procedure detail.

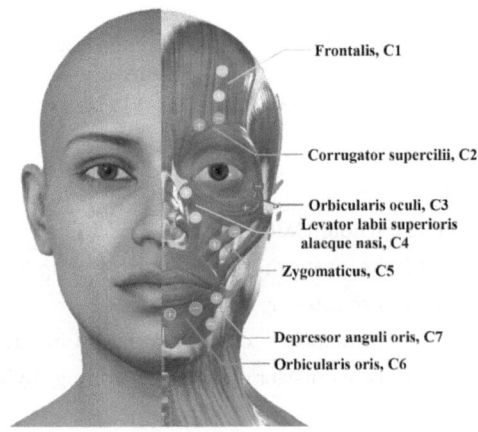

Fig. 2. Electrode distribution.

signals based on the audio content. Specifically, we identified five key time points during the question and answer (Q&A) sessions: t1, t2, t3, and t4, representing the start and end of questions and answers, as shown in Fig. 3. These time points were used to extract the corresponding Q&A EMG signal segments. Subsequently, based on the true responses of the completed questionnaire, we labeled each Q&A EMG segment as truth-telling and lying.

Next, in order to analyze the EMG signal changes before, during and after lying, we subdivided each Q&A EMG signal segment into four phases, i.e., in-question (P1), pre-answer (P2), in-answer (P3) and post-answer (P4). The correspondence between the phases and the time periods are listed in Table 1.

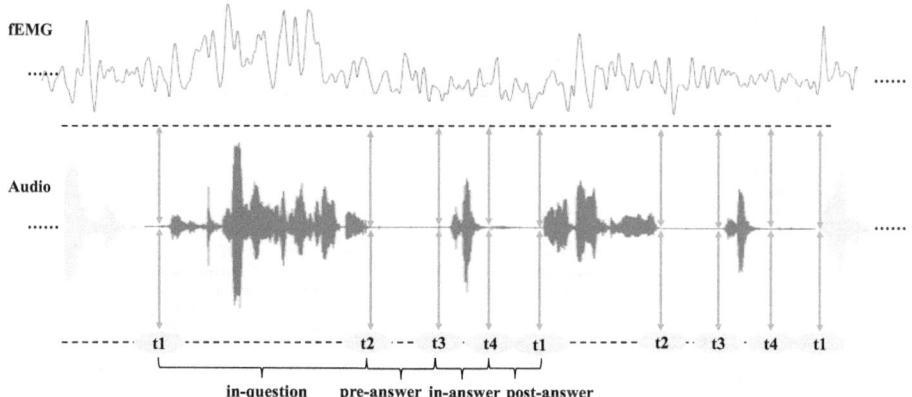

Fig. 3. Segmentation of the EMG signal through the time points obtained from the audio information.

Table 1. The phases correspond to specific time periods. The stage before truth-telling or lying includes the interrogee's information-receiving phase (in-question, P1) and the preparation phase for answering (pre-answer, P2). $t1_N$ denotes the start of the next Q&A session.

Index	Time	Phase	Label stage
P0	t1-$t1_N$	whole Q&A	Truth-telling/Lying
P1	t1-t2	in-question	before Truth-telling/Lying
P2	t2-t3	pre-answer	
P3	t3-t4	in-answer	during Truth-telling/Lying
P4	t4-$t1_N$	post-answer	after Truth-telling/Lying

In addition, in order to eliminate the impact of the sequence effect on the subsequent analysis, we randomly shuffled the EMG signal segments of truth-telling and lying.

3.3   Data Pre-processing

After acquiring and segmenting the EMG signal, we performed pre-processing to address interference from direct current (DC) and noise present in the raw data. Additionally, individual differences led to varying EMG signal amplitudes across participants. The varying durations of each Q&A segment also required standardization to facilitate subsequent machine learning analysis.

Signal Processing-Based EMG Signal Extraction. This subsection describes how to extract the specific EMG signals that reflect the facial muscle movements from the collected EMG raw data.

In the EMG acquisition process, the EMG device converts the electrical signal into a machine-analyzable digital signal after it is acquired. During this process, the DC would affects the EMG signals. Thus, we need to remove the DC offset at first. Specifically, the DC offset can be replaced by the mean value of the raw EMG signal x^{raw}, as shown in Eq. 1.

$$x_k^{\mathrm{r\_dc}} = x_k^{\mathrm{raw}} - \frac{1}{n} \sum_{i=1}^{n} x_i^{\mathrm{raw}} \tag{1}$$

where $k \in [1, n]$, n represents the length of the EMG signal. $x^{\mathrm{r\_dc}}$ represents the EMG signal after removing the DC offset.

To filter out noise and extract the EMG signal within the effective frequency band, we applied Butterworth filters, which are commonly used in EMG signal processing for their ability to preserve useful information. Specifically, due to the presence of 50 Hz power-line interference during the experiment, we set the cut-off frequencies of the bandstop Butterworth filter to 48 Hz and 52 Hz to eliminate the noise [28]. The filtered EMG signal, $x^{\mathrm{r\_n}}$, was obtained using Eq. 2.

$$x^{\mathrm{r\_n}} = \mathrm{Butterworth}(x^{\mathrm{r\_dc}}, [48\ \mathrm{Hz}, 52\ \mathrm{Hz}], \mathrm{stop}) \tag{2}$$

where $\mathrm{Butterworth}(u_1, u_2, u_3)$ is a bandpass or bandstop Butterworth filter. Specifically, u_1 represents the input sequence; u_2 indicates frequency range; and u_3 represents type of filter (bandpass or bandstop).

Then, the cut-off frequency of the bandpass Butterworth filter on signal $x^{\mathrm{r\_n}}$ was set to 20 Hz and 450 Hz for filtering the EMG signal x^{f} representing muscle movement [27].

$$x^{\mathrm{f}} = \mathrm{Butterworth}(x^{\mathrm{r\_n}}, [20\ \mathrm{Hz}, 450\ \mathrm{Hz}], \mathrm{pass}) \tag{3}$$

The absolute value of x^{f} was retained for full-wave rectification, as shown in Eq. 4 (where $\mathrm{abs}(\cdot)$ denotes the absolute value operation). Since muscle activity is reflected in the amplitude variation of the EMG signal, we then applied an envelope to the signal, resulting in the final EMG signal analyzed in this study.

$$x^{E} = \mathrm{Envelop}(\mathrm{abs}(x^{\mathrm{f}})) \tag{4}$$

where the operation $\mathrm{Envelop}(\cdot)$ returns the envelopes of the input sequence.

Feature Construction. In this subsection, we focus on how to construct features for lie detection analysis based on EMG signals, including outlier removal, normalization and dimension reduction.

Outlier Removal
As we introduced in Subsect. 3.2, the EMG signals were segmented corresponding to each Q&A session. The duration of each EMG segment is different because the content length and the participants' speech tempo may vary across Q&A sessions. As illustrated in Fig. 4, the longest duration of the sample is 19.2 s, and

the shortest is 1.3 s. To eliminate the impact of extreme length on the analysis, we used the PauTa Criterion, i.e., 3σ Criterion [6], to remove abnormal samples, as shown in Eq. 5.

$$\mu = \frac{1}{N}\sum_{k=1}^{N} d_k, \quad \sigma = \sqrt{\frac{1}{N}\sum_{k=1}^{N}(d_k - \mu)^2} \tag{5}$$

where N denotes the total Q&A session amount, $N = 1055$, d_k represents the kth sample duration. μ and σ were calculated as the mean duration and the standard deviation. The sample duration outside the $\mu \pm 3\sigma$ interval were considered as outliers and should be eliminated. Finally, 955 EMG signal segments were conserved for subsequent analysis. Furthermore, as previously described, we acquired EMG signal from seven channels simultaneously. Thus, for each EMG segment, there were seven channels of EMG signals.

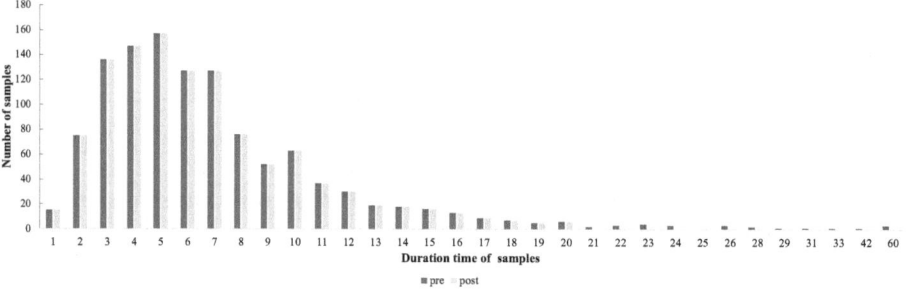

Fig. 4. EMG sample duration distribution.

Normalization

In the subsequent machine learning analysis, the model's input features need to have a uniform length. To achieve this, we normalized the EMG segment lengths using linear Fast Fourier Transform (FFT) interpolation, with the longest sample as the baseline [18].

In this study, we not only analyzed lie detection using the overall EMG signal during the Q&A session (P0) but also examined the impact of EMG signals in different Q&A sub-phases. Based on Table 1, we performed interpolation normalization (Eqs. 6 and 7) for the whole session and its four phases: P0, P1, P2, P3, and P4. The resulting interpolated EMG features I are presented in Table 2.

$$p_{i,j} = \max[\text{len}(x_{i,1}^{E}), ..., \text{len}(x_{i,6685}^{E})] - \text{len}(x_{i,j}^{E}) \tag{6}$$
$$I_{i,j} = \text{interpft}(x_{i,j}^{E}, p_{i,j}) \tag{7}$$

where $i \in [1,5]$ represents the entire segment and the four individual phases; $j \in [1, 6685]$ corresponds to the 6685 EMG signal segments, with each segment comprising seven channels of EMG signals. The functions len($\cdot$), max[$\cdot$], and interpft($\cdot$) denote operations for calculating length, maximum value, and linear FFT interpolation, respectively. $x_{i,j}^{E}$ represents the jth EMG signal of the ith phase, $p_{i,j}$ is the number of interpolation points, and $I_{i,j}$ represents the interpolated jth EMG feature of the ith phase.

Table 2. Interpolated EMG Feature Length for different Q&A phases.

Phase	P0	P1	P2	P3	P4
I Length	14768	2823	1737	567	9641

Dimension Reduction: The interpolated EMG features had high dimensionality, which could prolong the model training process and increase demands on computational resources. To mitigate this, we applied dimensionality reduction by removing irrelevant elements and retaining the most representative components for classification. Specifically, we used PCA to reduce feature dimensions, setting the retained energy value at 99.99

3.4   Machine Learning Methods

We aimed to verify whether computational algorithms can effectively learn features from EMG signals to detect lying. To assess learning efficiency, we compared two traditional machine learning models and one deep learning model.

Among the 955 EMG segments, 645 were truth-telling and 310 were lying, with consistent labeling across seven channels in each segment. Additionally, as shown in Eq. 8, EMG features from different phases were input into the models separately, enabling analysis of the importance of each phase for lie detection based on classification results.

$$Y_i^m = \text{Model}_m(X_i) \tag{8}$$

where $i \in [1, 5]$, indicates the whole and the four phases: P0, P1, P2, P3 and P4; $m \in [1, 3]$, Model_m indicates the SVM, RUSBoost tree and ResNet, respectively. X_i and Y_i^m represent the input and output of the Model_m.

Notably, the traditional models use one-dimensional temporal EMG signals that have been interpolated and reduced in dimensionality. In contrast, the deep learning model utilizes two-dimensional spectrograms representing time-frequency domain changes in the EMG signal. To preserve frequency domain information, no interpolation or dimensionality reduction was applied to the EMG signal before generating the spectrograms.

SVM (Temporal Domain). For SVM, the input X_i is the interpolated and downscaled EMG feature F. Since uneven distribution of samples would affect the performance of the classifier, in addition to the experiment on all samples, we also conducted an experiment with the equal amounts of samples in both classes (lying and truth-telling).

RUSBoosted Tree (Temporal Domain). For the RUSBoosted tree, which excels in handling unbalanced samples, we used all interpolated and downscaled EMG features F as input X_i. As shown in Subsect. 4.2, the RUSBoosted tree outperformed the other two models. Using this model, we classified lying and truth-telling based on the features of each EMG channel and various channel combinations. This approach allowed us to assess the relevance of muscle movements across different channels for lie detection.

ResNet (Time-Frequency Domain). For the deep learning model, we selected ResNet, commonly used in image classification and target detection. Since ResNet requires a two-dimensional input, spectrograms were fed into the network. While deeper ResNet layers offer higher feature abstraction, they increase training time and slow convergence. To mitigate this, we employed transfer learning, initializing the model with parameters from a pre-trained ResNet34, ensuring fast and stable training. Spectrograms were scaled to 256×256 pixels and center-cropped to 224×224. During training, a learning rate of 0.01 and a batch size of 16 were used. This configuration enhances training speed and accelerates convergence through parallel processing.

For evaluating classification results, we used 10-fold cross-validation. In this method, all features were divided into ten folds; nine were used for training, and one for testing. The model's accuracy was calculated using Eq. 9, where lying and truth-telling are the positive and negative conditions, respectively. TP_n and TN_n represent the number of true positives (TPs) and true negatives (TNs) in the classification results. Additionally, we assessed the model's performance using the AUC (area under the curve), providing a metric to measure the quality of the model's predictions.

$$\text{Accuracy} = \frac{\sum_{n=1}^{N}(\mathrm{TP}_n + \mathrm{TN}_n)}{\text{Sample amount}} \tag{9}$$

4 Results and Discussion

4.1 Statistic Analysis

In this section, we separately introduced the results of lie detection by humans through visual face-to-face observation, as well as the statistical analysis results based on EMG.

After conducting statistical analysis, we discovered that the accuracy of human judges in differentiating between truth-telling and lying is 49.26%, which is essentially equivalent to random level. This outcome is in line with the majority of prior research [5]. Furthermore, we conducted a more detailed analysis of the accuracy in successful lie detection within the deceptive samples, which was found to be 33.86%, indicating a performance lower than the random level.

We analyzed the obtained EMG signal x^E using SPSS Statistics 26. First, we conducted Independent Sample T-Test on the truth-telling and lying samples in

P0. As shown in Table 3, the results indicated that all channels were statistically significant difference except for C5. Moreover, in C1, C2, and C7, the EMG during lying were significantly higher than truth-telling. Conversely, in C3, C4, and C6, the EMG during truth-telling were significantly higher than lying.

Table 3. Independent Samples T Test In P0 (Q&A session). M represents mean value; SD represents standard deviation value; * represents $p< 0.05$. ** represents $p< 0.01$.

Channel	EMG(M± SD)		t	p
	truth-telling	lying		
C1	1.07±36.21	1.15±41.40	3.137	0.002**
C2	0.93±30.80	1.18±34.81	11.794	0.000**
C3	1.06±40.79	0.96±24.92	−5.528	0.000**
C4	1.05±35.03	0.86±26.14	−10.189	0.000**
C5	1.30±44.94	1.27±39.13	−1.095	0.274
C6	1.34±46.73	1.09±22.71	−12.184	0.000**
C7	1.18±43.25	1.45±45.03	9.872	0.000**

At the same time, we conducted participant-based analysis on the data in P0 using Paired Sample T-Test, which showed significant differences in C2 and C7. The EMG of C2 was significantly higher during lying (M = 1.38, SD = 2.27) than truth-telling (M = 0.79, SD= 1.63), t (15) = 2.33, p = 0.03* ($p< 0.05$), and the EMG of C7 was also significantly higher during lying (M = 1.79, SD = 2.84) than truth-telling (M = 1.09, SD = 1.71), t (15) = 2.22, p = 0.04* ($p< 0.05$).

4.2 Lie Detection Performance Based on Machine Learning

In this sub-section, we analyzed the performance of three EMG signal-based machine learning models for lie detection. Then, we explored the importance of different Q&A phases and facial muscles for lie detection.

Model Performance. The Table 4 presented the accuracies and AUCs of the three models, i.e., SVM, RUSBoosted tree and ResNet.

The SVM model was tested with two input cases due to concerns about the impact of unbalanced sample distributions. The first case used all available samples for training and testing (SVM_All), while the second used a balanced set of 310 lying and 310 truth-telling segments across 7 EMG channels (SVM_Equal). SVM_All achieved the highest accuracy, but its AUC was below 0.5, as shown in Fig. 5. SVM, being a nonlinear, high-dimensional model, performed well on the majority class, boosting overall accuracy. However, SVM's sensitivity to data imbalance resulted in poor learning of the minority class (truth-telling), reflected in the low AUC. For SVM_Equal, the balanced sample distribution reduced accuracy but improved AUC by decreasing the FPR.

Table 4. Peformance comparison among SVM, RUSBoosted tree and the ResNet. The SVM has two types of sample inputs, one with all samples used for training and testing (All), and the other with an equal number of samples for lying and truth-telling (Equal). Acc represents Accuracy(%). The best results are highlighted in bold.

Models		P0		P1		P2		P3		P4	
		Acc	AUC	Acc	AUC	Acc	AUC	Acc	AUC	Acc	AUC
SVM	All	**67.2**	0.49±0.06	64.6	0.46±0.02	64.5	0.45±0.03	66.0	0.48±0.01	64.2	0.46±0.02
	Equal	56.0	**0.55±0.01**	53.6	0.51±0.03	53.7	0.52±0.02	55.5	0.53±0.01	54.3	0.52±0.01
RUSBoosted tree		63.8	**0.69±0.01**	60.5	0.64±0.02	60.0	0.63±0.01	62.1	0.68±0.01	61.2	0.65±0.01
ResNet		**61.0**	0.66±0.01	56.5	0.60±0.03	58.1	0.63±0.03	59.5	0.65±0.01	57.6	0.63±0.02

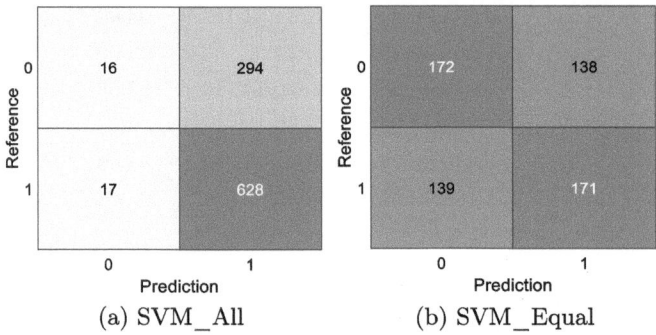

(a) SVM_All   (b) SVM_Equal

Fig. 5. Confusion matrix for SVM classifier with two input cases. 0 and 1 indicate the negative (truth-telling) and positive (lying) samples, respectively.

Secondly, for RUSBoosted tree, it is able to handle the data imbalance well compared to SVM since it models the minority class better by removing the majority class samples. Therefore, it obtained the highest AUC value and the accuracy is moderately acceptable.

Finally, for the deep learning model, theoretically, the deep learning network is able to learn the features of the samples more deeply, and therefore should have better results. However, compared to traditional machine learning models, ResNet did not achieve the expected results. These results may be due to the small number of samples in our experiments, while ResNet usually requires a large amount of data for training.

Importance of Different Q&A Phases for Lie Detection. Because RUS-Boosted tree classification had the best overall performance, we chose it for the subsequent analysis. Figure 6 and Fig. 7 show the lie detection results of classifiers trained with EMG features from different muscle or muscle combinations under different Q&A phases.

From Table 4, Fig. 6 and Fig. 7, it can be seen that the overall phase P0 had the highest performance of lie detection because it contains the most information, i.e., the facial muscle movements during the whole Q&A session.

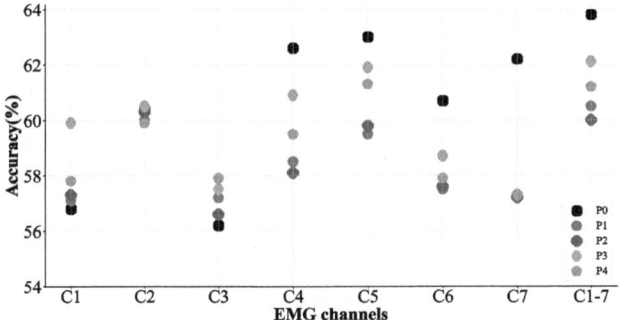

(a) Scatter plot shows lie detection performance in different phases with different EMG channels.

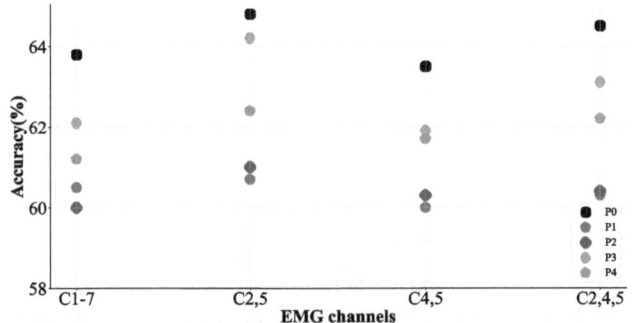

(b) Scatter plot shows lie detection performance in different phases with different EMG channel combinations.

Fig. 6. Lie detection comparison (Accuracy%) among different EMG channels and different Q&A phases - Scatter plots.

Specifically for the different phases of lie detection, the phase P3 had the best performance. This is because P3 corresponds to the phase of answering questions, which is the key stage when the interrogee express information to the interrogator and when facial movements are the most abundant. The features at this phase are the most discriminative, which is why the model is able to distinguish well between lying and truth-telling.

The performance of lie detection based on the P1 and P2 is the poorest. This two phases reflect the facial muscle movements of the interrogee before answering the question. The interrogees were more engaged in thinking rather than expressing. Therefore, the facial EMG in this phase contains the least action information.

For the P4, the facial movements in this phase are significantly reduced compared to P3. The EMG features of P4 may contain movements started at P3 that have not yet ended, or micro-expressions leaked without willing to be caught in a

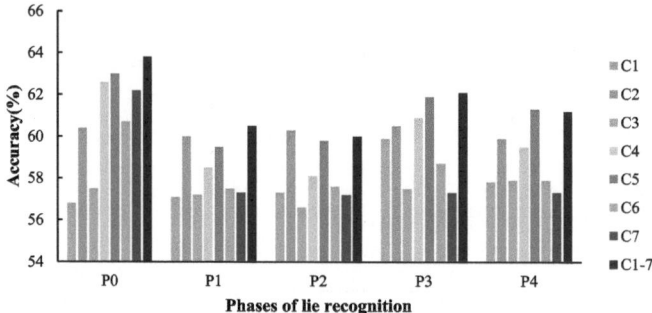

(a) Histogram shows lie detection performance of different single EMG channels at different phases.

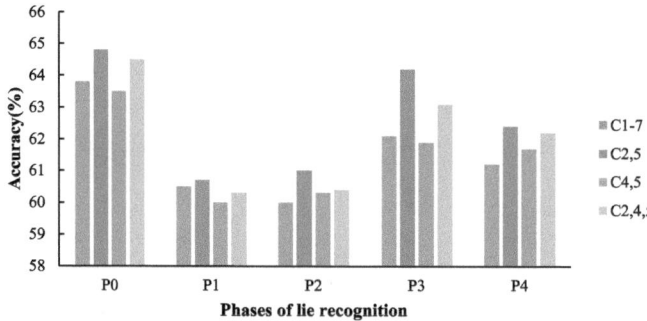

(b) Histogram shows lie detection performance of different EMG channel combinations at different phases.

Fig. 7. Lie detection comparison (Accuracy%) among different EMG channels and different Q&A phases - Histograms.

lie. The discrimination of these features is degraded. Therefore, the performance of lie detection based on P4 is lower than that of P3.

Importance of Different Facial Muscles for Lie Detection. Figure 6 and Fig. 7 illustrate that for any of the Q&A phases, the lie detection performance is best when all channels of EMG features are fed into the model. This is because facial expressions tend to involve muscle actions in most regions of the face. When information from all channels is employed, the model is able to comprehensively learn the features relevant to lying.

Lie detection performance varied across EMG channels, with C2, C4, and C5 outperforming others. This aligns with the lie detection-related facial EMG regions identified by Dong et al. [8]. Movements in the corrugator supercilii (C2), levator labii superioris alaeque nasi (C4), and zygomaticus (C5) provided crucial cues for the model. Notably, the C7 channel, which tracks depressor anguli oris movements, showed a different accuracy trend across phases. While C7 performed well in the overall phase P0-due to mouth movements providing verbal cues-its accuracy declined in sub-phases. This decline was due to limited mouth movements in phases P1, P2, and P4, and excessive interference from talking movements in phase P3.

Facial movements typically involve multiple muscles, not just single ones. To capture this complexity, we combined EMG features from channels C2, C4, and C5 in various permutations and used them as model inputs. The results, shown in Figs. 6b and 7b, indicate that the C2 and C5 combination achieved the highest accuracy, even surpassing the full-channel combination. This suggests that C2 and C5 provide the most relevant cues for detecting lies. Interestingly, adding more channels, like C2, C4, and C5 together, led to decreased model performance, implying that other channels may introduce noise rather than helpful information. These findings highlight the importance of focusing on Corrugator supercilii (C2) and Zygomaticus (C5) for lie detection using machine learning. Concentrating on these facial regions can enhance the accuracy and efficiency of models designed to detect lies based on physiological signals or visual data.

5 Conclusions

In our study, we showcased how statistics analysis and machine learning perform in recognizing intentional-deception. Statistics analysis provides some insights into the cognitive process of lying and the appearance of micro-expressions. Machine learning has revealed the different stages of lying and the importance of different facial muscles in lie detection. The integration of statistics analysis and machine learning has yielded valuable insights into the cognitive and physiological processes involved in lying. The experimental results also suggested that lie detection based on facial EMG signals can be an effective method for identifying deceptive behavior. Our study has shed light on the complex and multi-faceted nature of lying, and the challenges inherent in detecting deception. In addition, the potential for facial EMG signals to be used as a promising approach for future research in this area. As technology continues to advance, it is anticipated that the findings of this paper will contribute to the development of more sophisticated and accurate lie detection expert systems.

Acknowledgements. This work is supported, in part, by grants from the National Natural Science Foundation of China (62276252, 62106256), in part, by Research on the construction of social psychological service system for teenagers in the new era(23BSHJ01), and in part, by a grant from the Youth Innovation Promotion Association CAS.

References

1. Ang, L.B.P., Belen, E.F., Bernardo, R.A., Boongaling, E.R., Briones, G.H., Coronel, J.B.: Facial expression recognition through pattern analysis of facial muscle movements utilizing electromyogram sensors. In: 2004 IEEE Region 10 Conference TENCON 2004, vol. 100, pp. 600–603. IEEE (2004)

2. Bishop, C.M., Nasrabadi, N.M.: Pattern Recognition and Machine Learning, vol. 4. Springer, Heidelberg (2006)
3. Blair, J.P., Levine, T.R., Shaw, A.S.: Content in context improves deception detection accuracy. Hum. Commun. Res. **36**(3), 423–442 (2010)
4. Bond, G.D.: Deception detection expertise. Law Hum Behav. **32**(4), 339–351 (2008)
5. Bond, C.F., Jr., DePaulo, B.M.: Accuracy of deception judgments. Pers. Soc. Psychol. Rev. **10**(3), 214–234 (2006)
6. Chandola, V., Banerjee, A., Kumar, V.: Anomaly detection for discrete sequences: a survey. IEEE Trans. Knowl. Data Eng. **24**(5), 823–839 (2010)
7. DePaulo, B.M., Kashy, D.A., Kirkendol, S.E., Wyer, M.M., Epstein, J.A.: Lying in everyday life. J. Pers. Soc. Psychol. **70**(5), 979–995 (1996)
8. Dong, Z., Wang, G., Lu, S., Li, J., Yan, W., Wang, S.J.: Spontaneous facial expressions and micro-expressions coding: from brain to face. Front. Psychol. 5808 (2022)
9. Dopson, W.G., Beckwith, B.E., Tucker, D.M., Bullard-Bates, P.C.: Asymmetry of facial expression in spontaneous emotion. Cortex **20**(2), 243–251 (1984)
10. Edelstein, R.S., Luten, T.L., Ekman, P., Goodman, G.S.: Detecting lies in children and adults. Law Hum Behav. **30**(1), 1–10 (2006)
11. Ekman, P.: Darwin, deception, and facial expression. Ann. N. Y. Acad. Sci. **1000**(1), 205–221 (2003)
12. Ekman, P., Friesen, W.V.: Nonverbal leakage and clues to deception. Psychiatry **32**(1), 88–106 (1969)
13. Fricke, C., Alizadeh, J., Zakhary, N., Woost, T.B., Bogdan, M., Classen, J.: Evaluation of three machine learning algorithms for the automatic classification of emg patterns in gait disorders. Front. Neurol. **12**, 666458 (2021)
14. Girouard, M., Cavazos, J.E.: Electromyography-based seizure detector: preliminary results comparing a generalized tonic-clonic seizure detection algorithm to video-eeg recordings. Epilepsia **56**(9), 1432–1437 (2015)
15. Güler, N.F., Koçer, S.: Classification of emg signals using pca and fft. J. Med. Syst. **29**, 241–250 (2005)
16. Hurley, C.M., Anker, A.E., Frank, M.G., Matsumoto, D., Hwang, H.C.: Background factors predicting accuracy and improvement in micro expression recognition. Motiv. Emot. **38**(5), 700–714 (2014). https://doi.org/10.1007/s11031-014-9410-9
17. Joshi, D., Nakamura, B.H., Hahn, M.E.: High energy spectrogram with integrated prior knowledge for EMG-based locomotion classification. Med. Eng. Phys. **37**(5), 518–524 (2015)
18. Kim, H., Zhang, D., Kim, L., Im, C.H.: Classification of individual's discrete emotions reflected in facial microexpressions using electroencephalogram and facial electromyogram. Expert Syst. Appl. **188**, 116101 (2022)
19. Levine, T.R.: New and improved accuracy findings in deception detection research. Curr. Opin. Psychol. **6**, 1–5 (2015)
20. Li, J., et al.: CAS(ME)^3: a third generation facial spontaneous micro-expression database with depth information and high ecological validity. IEEE Trans. Pattern Anal. Mach. Intell. **45**(3), 2782–2800 (2023)
21. Luo, M., Hancock, J.T., Markowitz, D.M.: Credibility perceptions and detection accuracy of fake news headlines on social media: effects of truth-bias and endorsement cues. Commun. Res. **49**(2), 171–195 (2022)
22. Mac Giolla, E., Luke, T.J.: Does the cognitive approach to lie detection improve the accuracy of human observers? Appl. Cogn. Psychol. **35**(2), 385–392 (2021)

23. Owayjan, M., Kashour, A., Al Haddad, N., Fadel, M., Al Souki, G.: The design and development of a lie detection system using facial micro-expressions. In: 2012 2nd International Conference on Advances in Computational Tools for Engineering Applications (ACTEA), pp. 33–38. IEEE (2012)
24. Ozdemir, M.A., Kisa, D.H., Guren, O., Onan, A., Akan, A.: EMG based hand gesture recognition using deep learning. In: 2020 Medical Technologies Congress (TIPTEKNO), pp. 1–4. IEEE (2020)
25. O'Sullivan, M.: Emotional intelligence and deception detection: why most people can't "read" others, but a few can. In: Applications of Nonverbal Communication, pp. 215–253 (2005)
26. Porter, S., Ten Brinke, L., Wallace, B.: Secrets and lies: involuntary leakage in deceptive facial expressions as a function of emotional intensity. J. Nonverbal Behav. 36(1), 23–37 (2012)
27. Reaz, M., Hussain, M.S., Mohd-Yasin, F.: Techniques of emg signal analysis: detection, processing, classification and applications. Biol. Proc. Online 8(1), 11–35 (2006)
28. Sarwar, N., Sandhu, M.S., Ricketts, S.L., Butterworth, A.S., et al.: Triglyceride-mediated pathways and coronary disease: collaborative analysis of 101 studies. The Lancet 375(9726), 1634–1639 (2010)
29. Seiffert, C., Khoshgoftaar, T.M., Van Hulse, J., Napolitano, A.: Rusboost: a hybrid approach to alleviating class imbalance. IEEE Trans. Syst. Man Cybern.-Part A: Syst. Humans 40(1), 185–197 (2009)
30. Shuster, A., Inzelberg, L., Ossmy, O., Izakson, L., Hanein, Y., Levy, D.J.: Lie to my face: an electromyography approach to the study of deceptive behavior. Brain Behav. 11(12), e2386 (2021)
31. Srivastava, N., Dubey, S.: Deception detection using artificial neural network and support vector machine. In: 2018 Second International Conference on Electronics, Communication and Aerospace Technology (ICECA), pp. 1205–1208. IEEE (2018)
32. Ten Brinke, L., Lee, J.J., Carney, D.R.: Different physiological reactions when observing lies versus truths: initial evidence and an intervention to enhance accuracy. J. Pers. Soc. Psychol. 117(3), 560–578 (2019)
33. Vrij, A., Granhag, P.A., Porter, S.: Pitfalls and opportunities in nonverbal and verbal lie detection. Psychol. Sci. Public Interest 11(3), 89–121 (2010)
34. Wagner-Altendorf, T.A., et al.: The electrocortical signature of successful and unsuccessful deception in a face-to-face social interaction. Front. Hum. Neurosci. 14, 277 (2020)
35. Zawawi, T.T., Abdullah, A.R., Shair, E.F., Halim, I., Rawaida, O.: Electromyography signal analysis using spectrogram. In: 2013 IEEE Student Conference on Research and Development, pp. 319–324. IEEE (2013)

Application Track

An Adaptive Hot Ranking Algorithm for Popular Item Recommendation in the Express Industry

Bohan Li[1] , Qingwei Zeng[1], Pan Ren[1(✉)], Huan Chen[1], Yankun Geng[1], and Liang-Jie Zhang[2]

[1] SF Technology, Shenzhen, China
{libohan1,panren}@sf-express.com
[2] ShenZhen University, Shenzhen, China

Abstract. Within the scope of recommendation systems, content-based and collaborative filtering recommendations encounter difficulties when dealing with the cold start, particularly when considering the temporal evolution of item popularity. These algorithms tend to recommend highly popular items, neglecting the dynamic nature of item hotness over time. In the express industry, users independently choose items for delivery, and many of these items exhibit seasonal patterns. Traditional recommendation methods may struggle to effectively capture the current popular items.To address the cold start issue in express item recommendation, this paper introduces an adaptive hot items ranking value (ADHV) algorithm. This algorithm accounts for temporal changes in express item volume and overall popularity. It adjusts the base hot value of each item using Bayesian ideas to determine its true hotness.This paper also proposes a metric called Hot Item Weighted Evaluation (HWE) to address the issue of the inability to quantitatively evaluate cold start recommendations. The HWE metric combines Newton's cooling method with Spearman's idea. The experimental results compare different hot ranking recommendations algorithms, and the HWE metric confirms the effectiveness and robustness of the ADHV algorithm.

Keywords: Hot item · Recommendation · Cold start problem · Bayesian average

1 Introduction

Traditional recommendation system algorithms generally rely on users' historical characteristics, such as ratings and purchase records, to construct user's profiles and generate recommendations. Currently, although content-based recommendation systems, collaborative filtering-based recommendation systems and hybrid recommendation systems are popular recommendation techniques [2]. These methods require users' long-term historical behavior preferences and their interaction with different items [5]. However, once lacking or missing the data of users' behaviour, especially when users are anonymous or visiting the system for the first time, the accuracy of recommendations is significantly impaired [4, 8, 24]. In express industry, delivering items is always a temporary

R. Xu et al. (Eds.): ICCC 2024, LNCS 15426, pp. 71–87, 2025.
https://doi.org/10.1007/978-3-031-77954-1_5

behavior with a clear intention. There is no historical preference information that can be followed. Therefore, long-term preference recommendation algorithms are unreliable and it is necessary to use short-term item metadata information to capture users' order intentions [13]. To solve the problem that anonymous users cannot use historical preference for recommendations, Session-based Recommendation (SBR) was proposed. SBR mainly focuses on users' recent sending behavior while does not rely too much on historical preference, thereby providing users with more accurate and timely recommendations [23].

However, many SBR models have a popularity bias problem and tend to recommend high popularity items[23]. This may not have business application value in many fields. The popularity trend of express items is changed over time and always exhibits seasonal characteristics such as fresh food and new electronic products. Therefore, we prefer to recommend items that have a certain popularity and a significant growth of popularity trend [1, 16]. Some researchers have studied the popularity bias problem [14, 26]. On the one hand, content-based similarity can be used to rank and recommend long-tail items [11, 19]. On the other hand, the popularity trend of items can be predicted based on time information [12, 19]. Regarding the recommendation results of long-tail items, it is difficult to explain the performance of the recommendation algorithm through quantitative indicators. Traditional evaluation indicators such as accuracy, recall, and Mean Reciprocal Rank (MRR) will score higher for high-popularity items, and the scores will drop in long-tail recommendations. Harald et al. [20] proposed a measurement indicator that can balance the popularity and accuracy of recommended items, allowing long-tail recommendations to be reasonably explained. In addition, Herlocker et al. [9] and Andrew et al. [18] proposed the use of Receiver Operator Characteristic (ROC) curves as an evaluation of recommendations, including Global Roc (GROC) and Customer Roc (CROC). These two evaluation indicators can measure the accuracy of heuristic recommender systems when recommending items to different users.

In this paper, we propose a express recommendation ranking algorithm in the logistics field. By considering the trend of changes in the order scale of express items over time, and combining the idea of Bayesian averaging, this algorithm can balance the relationship between the popularity and growth rate of express items, thereby focusing more on recommending popular long-tail items, and adaptively offering the top N recommendation list of item popularity. In addition, based on the concept of hot topics, we propose an evaluation indicator that can quantify the long-tail recommendation algorithm. This evaluation indicator combines the Spearman algorithm and Newton cooling idea, calculates the ranking information given by each algorithm over time, and obtains the reliability of the top N ranking according to the ranking relevance at different recommendation moments. This evaluation indicator can give long-tail items a higher recommendation score, so it can reasonably quantify the results of the popularity bias recommendation algorithm. Finally, based on the real logistics consignment dataset, this article verifies the proposed recommendation algorithm and other existing recommendation ranking algorithms. Through the change of daily express volume, the effectiveness and rationality of the proposed recommendation algorithm and evaluation indicators are assessed (Fig. 1).

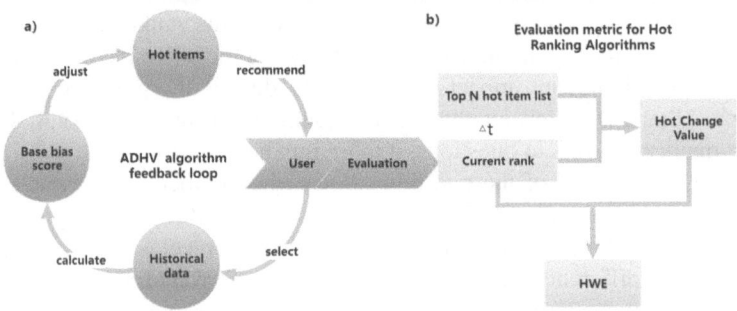

Fig. 1. Flowchart on ADHV algorithm (a) and hot ranking recommendation evaluation (b)

2 Related Work

What is a Hot Item? As suggested by by Bun et al. [3] and and Kuan et al. [10], the researchers provide definitions and descriptions of "hot topic" that has a high level of popularity over a period of time. In journalism, hot topics need to consider how often the term appears and how its popularity changes over time [22]. In the express industry, the "hotness" of products also need to be considered. In summary, the descriptions of the "hot item" is given in this paper as follows:

- The popularity of an item grows rapidly over a certain period of time.
- The popularity of an item should be above a certain threshold for a certain period of time.
- The popularity of an item will decrease over time.

Most of current hots item ranking algorithms use user's activity, clicks, comments, and other indicators for a particular topic as the basis for determining hotness for ranking and recommendation [7].The frequency method is one of the most basic statistical methods that determines the importance of each hot item by counting the frequency of its occurrence in historical application scenarios, with items that occur more frequently being considered more important. The method is very intuitive and easy to calculate, but it does not reflect the trend of the item's hotness over time [21].

In order to obtain more accurate hot items, many researchers have optimized and improved the algorithm on the frequency. The hot item recommendation of many websites is based on the frequency method, which introduces time, positive and negative feedback from users and other information as derivative features to eliminate the "Matthew effect" to solve the cold start problem. The "Matthew effect" refers to the phenomenon where the strong become stronger and the weak become weaker. Mario et al. [6] proposed a novel topic detection technique retrieve in realtime the most emergent topics expressed by the community based on temporal and social terms. Xue et al. [25] introduced a method which combined frequency and time series to detect hot items in microblogs by calculating the growth slope. Reddit is a very large online community in the United States where posts are sorted according to user votes. The algorithm combines information about time and the number of votes for and against a post. Content that has received a lot of positive feedback in a recent period will rise in the rankings, and will gradually fall over time if there is no new feedback. However, negative feedback in the early stages can have a significant impact on the results, despite the presence of numerous positive votes. Stack Overflow emphasizes the quality of professional Q&A. To recommend high-quality answers to questions, it takes into account various dimensions, such as the current time period of the question ratings, the number of views, discussions, and other relevant information [17]. Newton's Law of Cooling is a sorting algorithm inspired by physics. It states that the rate of cooling of an object is directly proportional to the temperature difference between the object and its surroundings. In the context of ranking hot items, it can be interpreted as follows: the hotter an item is compared to its historical hotness, the faster its hotness will decrease. Therefore, by establishing a time window, the cooling coefficient can be used to indicate the trend of the object's hot level, it is rising or falling. The formula is as follows:

$$\text{Newton} = \ln(\frac{Hotness_{t1} + 1}{Hotness_{t0} + 1})/\Delta t. \tag{1}$$

The Bayesian Average method is used to calculate movie ratings for MDB TOP250 [15, 17]. It is designed to address the issue of longtail items not being recommended. The method involves giving a base score based on existing voting results of the item, and then continuously correcting the ranking score of the item with changes in votes to make the final score closer to the actual value. The formula for the Bayesian Average is as follows:

$$\text{BA} = \frac{swf}{swf + aswf} \times rs + \frac{aswf}{swf + aswf} \times ars, \tag{2}$$

where

- swf is the real current hot value for the item i.
- $aswf$ is the global hot value for all items.
- rs is base hot value for the item i.
- ars is average base hot value for the all items.

These methods can be selected or used in combination based on specific application scenarios. In the empirical analysis section, the results of different sorting recommendation algorithms will be compared based on the hot products recommendation scenarios for sending goods in the express industry.

3 The Adaptive Hot Item Ranking Value

In this section, the Adaptive Hot Word Ranking algorithm (ADHV) is proposed. It is a weighted algorithm that takes the base hot value of each candidate item as a prior information and corrects it according to the current hot value to obtain a score that more accurately represents the change of the candidate item over time.

3.1 Base Hot Value

The user's selection can determine the hotness of an item, while the base hot score is equivalent to the a prior information, which can reflect the popularity growth of each item. It can obtain a relatively fairer and more reasonable score for some candidate items with low initial popularity but high growth in a short time. Specifically, the Base Hot Score BH_i for each item can be expressed as follows:

$$
\begin{aligned}
BH_i &= \exp(\tfrac{DH_i}{SH_i}), \\
DH_i &= CHi - HH_i, \\
SH_i &= CHi + HH_i,
\end{aligned}
\tag{3}
$$

where

- CHi is the current hot value(popularity) for the item i.
- HH_i is the history hot value(popularity) for the item i.
- DH_i is the difference hot value between CHi and HH_i.
- SH_i is the sum hot value between CHi and HH_i.

The hot value can be expressed in terms of popularity, which is determined by the number of selections made by users for the item. The base hot value is higher for smaller SH_i values with the same DH_i, creating a bias towards small popularity item. For the high popularity item, a larger DH_i is required to achieve the same BH_i as the small item. The exponential guarantees that BHi is greater than zero and monotonic at $(-\infty, +\infty)$. In this manner, even if the DH_i is negative, the exponential transformation can make the BH_i is positive, allowing the item to participate in ranking despite decreasing popularity.

3.2 Hot Weighting Factor

The recommendation ranking results also take into account the popularity of the candidate items in addition to the base hot value.

The hot weighting factor ω_i is used to adjust the base score to better balance the relationship between the popularity and the growth rate. For a candidate item, its hot weighting factor can be expressed as:

$$
\begin{aligned}
\omega_i &= \tfrac{DH_i}{CH_{avg}+CH_i}, \\
CH_{avg} &= \tfrac{\sum_{i\in I}CH_i}{n},
\end{aligned}
\tag{4}
$$

where CH_{avg} is the average of the CH_i of all candidate items. In the case of the same DH for different items, if the CH is higher, indicating that a higher HH, the change of hotness becomes less significant, which means a lower weight factor w. Likewise, in the case of the same CH, the higher the DH, the higher the w. For some less popular candidates, their low SH may lead to very high BH, thus creating unreliable rankings. By using the hot weighting factor, the reliability of the hotness of low popular candidate items can be greatly improved.

3.3   The Top-N Hot Items Recommendation Algorithm Design

According to the base score and weighting factors, the ADHV_i of a candidate word i can be expressed as follows:

$$\begin{aligned} \text{ADHV}_i &= \omega_i \times \text{BH}_i \\ &= \frac{\text{DH}_i}{\text{CH}_{avg}+\text{CH}_i} \times \text{BH}_i \end{aligned} \quad (5)$$

To obtain the top-N recommended hot items, the candidate items are sorted according to their ADHVs. The detailed calculation procedures are introduced below:

Algorithm 1 Calculating Hot Items Ranking

Input: Dataset for candidate items $I(i_1,\ldots,i_n)$;
      Current and historical time frame t;
      Ranking threshold N

Output: The top-N recommended hot items: $(\text{ADHV}_1,\ldots,\text{ADHV}_n)$

1.Count the hot values HH_i and CH_i of each candidate item i at the historical told and current t now moments based on user votes.
2.Calculate the BH_i and ω_i for each candidate item i based on Equation 3 and 4.
3.Calculate the ADHV_i via Equation 5 based on the BH_i and ω_i.
4.Based on the given ranking threshold N, outputs the top-N recommended hot items sorted by ADHVs.

Remark

ADHV has the following features:

- The metric is consistent with the definition of a hot item, taking into account its own and global popularity. It balances the relationship between historical and current hot values and the hot increase of candidate items. This metric gives a fairer ranking to candidate items that have grown rapidly in a short period of time, but have a low initial hotness.
- Compared to the Bayesian averaging algorithm, ADHV can be computed for all candidate items without filtering them by setting a popularity threshold. And items with decreasing popularity can also be included in the ranking.
- The algorithm also weights less popular items more appropriately, so that they are not over weighted by the average.

4   Evaluation of Ranking Algorithms for Recommending Hot Items

The recommendation metrics of most recommendation algorithms will give preference to items that have a higher popularity, such as accuracy and recall. However, these metrics may assign lower values to long-tail items, resulting in cold recommendations for long-tail items that cannot be reasonably evaluated. This paper proposes the Hot Item Weighted Evaluation (HWE) to assess the performance of hot item recommendation ranking algorithms based on Newton's Law of Cooling and Spearman Rank Correlation Coefficient. Based on the trend of ranking results over time, the HWE can evaluate the effectiveness and robustness of ranking algorithms for hot item recommendation.

4.1 Hot Change Value

Combined with the definition of the Hot Item, it is reasonable to assume that a hot item given at the moment $t0$ will still rank relatively high or have an upward trend in ranking after a small period of time Δt. Therefore, we propose the hot change value to reflect the degree of rise and fall of the hot information of the candidate items.

Suppose there are K recommendation algorithms, at the moment $t0$ each algorithm returns the top-N hot items as $(I_{11}, ..., I_{1N}), ..., (I_{K1}, ..., I_{KN})$, where I_{ij} is the ith method that gives a rank of the jth hot item. Given a time window Δt, the ranking of these hot items will change at the time $t_1 = t_0 + \Delta t$. The rankings of these items, recalculated according to the recommendation algorithm, are $(r_{11}, ..., r_{1N}), ..., (r_{K1}, ..., r_{KN})$. At these two moments, the ranking difference is $(r_{11} - 1, ..., r_{1N} - N), ..., (r_{K1} - 1, ..., r_{KN} - N)$ for each algorithm. For recommendation algorithm i, the hot change value of the candidate item I_{ij} is

$$H_{ij} = \frac{1}{j} \times \frac{1}{1 + \exp(r_{ij} - j)}. \tag{6}$$

Here we adopt the idea of Newton's law of cooling: the cooling rate of information is proportional to the difference between its current and initial hotness. Calculating the rank difference between two moments of a candidate item can reflect the cooling rate. Since the time window of each candidate item is the same, the larger the rank difference, the more significant the change in hot level. Real hot items will still rank relatively high or remain hot in a smaller window Δt. To ensure monotonicity and a metric range between 0 and 1, the *Sigmoid* function is chosen to calculate the ranking trend change of hot items. The $1/j$ is the ranking adjustment factor. For candidates with the same change in ranking trend, if an item is ranked j higher at the initial moment t_0 then it has a higher hot change value.

4.2 Hot Item Weighted Evaluation

The weighted evaluation of the different recommendation algorithms is calculated after the hot change values are given. It is expected that there is a positive correlation between the hot change value and the current ranking of recommended hot items. The Spearman rank correlation coefficient is used to measure the correlation between two variables with rank nature. In this case, the hot change scores of the recommended times given by each recommendation algorithm are calculated and then sorted to obtain the rank of the hot change scores of the recommended words given by each algorithm. The Spearman correlation coefficient between the recommendation ranking result and the hot change value rank of each algorithm at the moment t_0 is then calculated below:

$$s_i = 1 - \frac{6 \times \sum_{j=1}^{N} d_j^2}{N(N^2 - 1)} \tag{7}$$

where the d_j represents the difference between the recommend rank of candidate j at the moment t_0 and its hot change value order. A value of s_i closer to 1 indicates a stronger correlation and more reliable ranking of hot items. According to Eqs. 6 and 7, the Hot Weight Evaluation(HWE) is calculated for each recommendation algorithm:

$$\text{HWE}_i = s_i \times \sum_{j=1}^{N} H_{ij} \tag{8}$$

For each recommendation algorithm, HWE is calculated separately. The larger HWE indicates that the overall trend of the hotness of the recommended results given by the algorithm is more in line with the characteristics of hot items, and the better the recommendation effect is.

5 Experiments

In this section, we validate the ADHV algorithm and HWE metric proposed in this paper by using real-world user ordering data from the logistics industry. The dataset was obtained from the SF Express app and includes the number of consignments for fresh items placed by users on September 2023. The change occurred before the Mid-Autumn Festival, which better reflects the seasonal trend of order hotness for items. After preprocessing the data, we obtained 141 canonical candidate items for sent items. Based on the seasonal characteristics of fresh food and the law of delivery, the time window between current time t_1 and historical time t_0 is set to three days (Table 1).

Table 1. ADHV algorithm results for top 10 recommended hot items on September 23rd. CH and HH are the orders placed on Sept. 22nd and Sept. 20th, and the CH$_{avg}$ is 47.377.

Candidate items	CH	HH	SH	DH	BH	ω	ADHV
Grapefruit	30	5	35	25	2.039	0.293	0.598
Shrimp	117	55	172	62	1.434	0.360	0.516
Guava	78	35	113	43	1.463	0.323	0.472
Kiwi	223	132	355	91	1.292	0.327	0.423
Mooncake	545	386	931	159	1.186	0.265	0.314
Chicken	261	183	444	78	1.192	0.247	0.294
Goose	11	2	13	9	1.988	0.136	0.270
Beef	344	252	596	92	1.167	0.230	0.269
Matsutake	16	5	21	11	1.684	0.154	0.260
Crab	350	262	612	88	1.155	0.217	0.251

5.1   Comparison of Hot Fresh Items Recommendations with Different Algorithms

We provide top-N recommended hot items for the ADHV algorithm based on users' historical consignments information. To demonstrate the recommendation effect clearly, we compare different recommendation ranking algorithms, including Bayesian Average method, Newton's law of Cooling, and Popularity algorithm. To better understand the ADHV algorithm, we give the calculation results of the top 10 recommended hot items of the ADHV on September 23rd.

Tables 2, 3 and 4 give the recommended consignments for different recommended algorithms on September 23rd, September 25th and September 30th, respectively. This time period is around the Mid Autumn Festival, and the change in the orders of fresh food consignments can be significantly observed. In order to directly compare the recommendation effect, we give the order quantity CH at time t_1, the order quantity HH at time t_0, and the order increment DH. It can be seen that the order trend of fresh consignments before the Mid-Autumn Festival is growing, but different algorithms give different hot items recommendations. By comparing the results of recommended hot items in Tables 2, 3 and 4, it can be found that on September 23rd and September 25th, ADHV and Bayesian algorithms give similar recommendation results because both algorithms take into account the hotness information of the global candidate recommendation items and correct the current popularity. The value of BH also shows that both algorithms capture consignments with low initial order volume but high incremental volume. In the recommended results on September 23rd, the ADHV algorithm gives "kiwi", "mooncake", "beef", "chicken" and "crab" as the most hot items which maintain a large order volume with a growing rate; "grapefruit", "shrimp", "guava", "goose" and "matsutake" are not the largest in terms of the historical order volume, but there is a significant increase in order (more than 100%) at the t_0 and t_1 moments. In particular, "grapefruit" saw a 500% increase in order volume. Although the increase in orders for "goose" was also 450%, respectively, due to small numbers of total orders, they were still ranked relatively low.

However, the recommendation results on September 30th, namely after the Mid-Autumn Festival, indicate a significant drop in order volume for many consignments. The Bayesian algorithm cannot accurately handle items that experience a drop in "hotness". Most recommended items at t_1 are less popular than at t_0, which is obviously unreasonable. However, the ADHV algorithm addresses this issue by incorporating consignments with a negative growth rate to the calculation of the hot item ranking. To analyse items with declined hotness, they can be arranged in the reverse order based on their rankings.

According to the recommendation results given by Newton's algorithm, it can be seen that the method only took into account the growth rate without considering the order volume of the consignment itself, resulting in the recommendation of the hot items that have large order growth rates but small order volume. For example, "blueberry", "orange" and "persimmon" that have small order volume, but fluctuated order growth rates are not suitable to be recommended as hot items on September 23rd. The popularity method only considers the order volume of consignments, which leads to the fact that consignments with high order volume will always be recommended, while the real hot items cannot be captured. And when the order volume of consignments drops, these consignments may also be recommended. From the recommendation data on September 30th, the Bayesian

Table 2. The top 10 recommended hot items given by different algorithms on Sept. 23rd.

ADHV	Grapefruit	Shrimp	Guava	Kiwi	Mooncake	Chicken	Goose	Beef	Matsutake	Crab
CH	30	117	78	223	545	261	11	344	16	350
HH	5	55	35	132	386	183	2	252	5	262
DH	25	62	43	91	159	78	9	92	11	88
Bayesian	**Shrimp**	**Guava**	**Grapefruit**	**Kiwi**	**Mooncake**	**Chicken**	**Beef**	**Prune**	**Crab**	**Matsutake**
CH	117	78	30	223	545	261	344	36	350	16
HH	55	35	5	132	386	183	252	20	262	5
DH	62	43	25	91	159	78	92	16	88	11
Newton	**Grapefruit**	**Goose**	**Beef steak**	**Passion fruit**	**Matsutake**	**Gooseberry**	**Blueberry**	**Orange**	**Persimmon**	**Lobster**
CH	30	11	6	8	16	9	4	4	4	10
HH	5	2	1	2	5	3	1	1	1	4
DH	25	9	5	6	11	6	3	3	3	6
Popularity	**Seafood**	**Pork**	**Mooncake**	**Apple**	**Fish**	**Grape**	**Beef**	**Chicken**	**Crab**	**Kiwi**
CH	773	518	545	523	435	449	344	261	350	223
HH	694	511	386	449	375	358	252	183	262	132
DH	79	7	159	74	60	91	92	78	88	91

Table 3. The top 10 recommended hot items given by different algorithms on Sept. 25th.

ADHV	Mooncake	Kiwi	Guava	Grapefruit	Chicken	Shrimp	Beef steak	Mutton	Winter jujube	Seafood
CH	13	422	161	77	419	187	22	174	71	970
HH	545	223	78	30	261	117	6	112	41	17
DH	608	199	83	47	158	70	16	62	30	197
Bayesian	**Mooncake**	**Kiwi**	**Guava**	**Grapefruit**	**Chicken**	**Shrimp**	**Mutton**	**Winter jujube**	**Beef steak**	**Mango**
CH	1153	422	161	77	419	187	174	71	22	34
HH	545	223	78	30	261	117	112	41	6	17
DH	608	199	83	47	158	70	62	30	16	17
Newton	**Flower**	**Beef steak**	**Cherry**	**Longan**	**Grapefruit**	**Rabbit**	**Vegetable**	**Abalone**	**Mooncake**	**Guava**
CH	6	22	5	10	77	6	6	8	1153	161
HH	1	6	1	3	30	2	2	3	545	78
DH	5	16	4	7	47	4	4	5	608	83
Popularity	**Mooncake**	**Seafood**	**Apple**	**Grape**	**Pork**	**Fish**	**Crab**	**Beef**	**Chicken**	**Kiwi**
CH	1153	970	624	526	529	448	424	432	419	422
HH	545	773	523	449	518	435	350	344	261	223
DH	608	197	101	77	11	13	74	88	158	199

Table 4. The top 10 recommended hot items given by different algorithms on Sept. 30th.

ADHV	Grapefruit	Cantaloupe	Leek	Corn	Beef offal	Strawberry	Tomato	Cherry	Seafood	Pineapple
CH	130	29	9	21	9	10	7	9	1686	6
HH	67	14	2	12	3	4	2	4	1545	2
DH	63	15	7	9	6	6	5	5	141	4
Bayesian	Grapefruit	Seafood	Cantaloupe	Crab	Corn	Apple	Leek	Strawberry	Beef offal	Cherry
nwf	130	1686	29	1105	21	783	9	10	9	9
hwf	67	1545	14	1189	12	865	2	4	3	4
dws	63	141	15	-84	9	-82	7	6	6	5
Newton	Leek	Tomato	Beef offal	Melon	Pineapple	Strawberry	Cantaloupe	Cherry	Water caltrop	Pineapple
CH	9	7	9	4	6	10	29	9	7	7
HH	2	2	3	1	2	4	14	4	3	3
DH	7	5	6	3	4	6	15	5	4	4
Popularity	Mooncake	Seafood	Crab	Apple	Grape	Chicken	Pork	Beef	Kiwi	Fish
CH	1120	1686	1105	783	488	461	540	511	375	294
HH	3116	1545	1189	865	981	813	689	670	579	561
DH	-1996	141	-84	-82	-493	-352	-149	-159	-204	-267

recommendation algorithm gives some consignments with declined order volume. Like "crab" and "apple", whose demand demand for shipping begins to decline after the Mid-Autumn Festival, so they should not be taken as hot items. Figures 2, 3 and 4 gives the change of order volume of top 5 hot items of different algorithms on September 23rd. Subplot (a) displays the trend of order volume change from 20th to 26th September for the recommended hot items and the green bar chart is the average daily order volume. Subplot (b) displays the growth rate for the items within the specified time window and the horizontal line represents the average growth rate of all candidate items. Comparing the volume and growth rate of hot items, it is clear that the growth rate of items identified by the ADHV and Bayesian is higher than average."Grapes" have grown at a rate of up to 5, despite a small initial order volume. All of these items meet the criteria for "hotness", indicating that the ADHV algorithm can adaptively identify hot items in the long-tail segment. Figure 3 displays the trend of the recommended hot items' hotness by the Newton method. Although the growth trend is evident, the orders are typically below average. The items recommended by the popularity method have a high daily order volume, but the growth rate varies consistently. Apart from "mooncake", the growth rate of the other recommended items did not exceed the average.

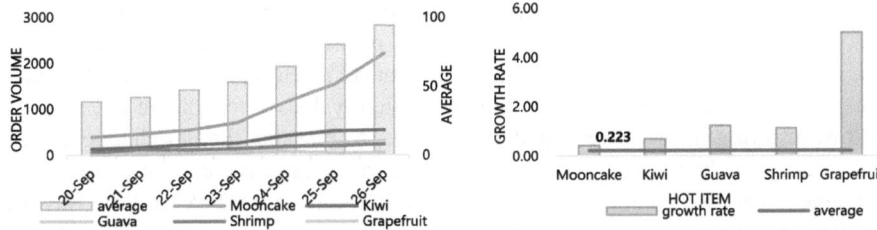

(a) Order volume change curve for top 5 recommended items by ADHV(Bayesian).

(b) Growth rates of the top 5 recommended items for the ADHV(Bayesian).

Fig. 2. Trends in the hotness of top 5 recommended items by the ADHV(Bayesian).

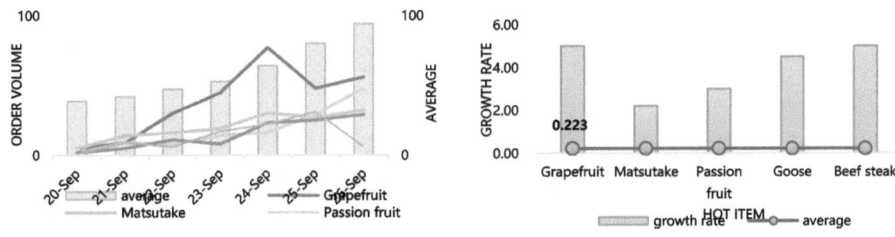

(a) Order volume change curve for top 5 recommended items by Newton.

(b) Growth rates of the top 5 recommended items for the Newton.

Fig. 3. Trends in the hotness of top 5 recommended items by the Newton

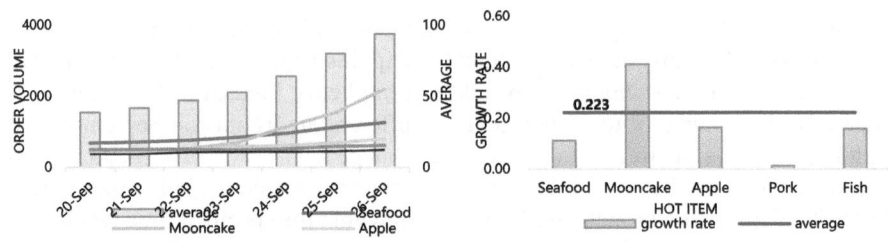

(a) Order volume change curve for top 5 recommended items by Popularity.

(b) Growth rates of the top 5 recommended items
for the Popularity.

Fig. 4. Trends in the hotness of top 5 recommended items by the Popularity.

5.2   Comparison of the HWE Metrics for Different Ranking Algorithms

To evaluate the effectiveness of hot item recommendations, we present the evaluation metrics for the ADHV, Bayesian, Newton and Popularity method based on the recommendation results of September 23rd and 25th. Tables 5 and 6 present the hot change values and HWE metrics for each algorithm.

From Tables 5 and 6, it can be seen that the ADHV algorithm has the highest HWE score. The Newton algorithm has the strongest positive correlation between the hot change value order and the hot ranking at the moment of t_0. However, due to the fluctuated ranking at the moments of t_0 and t_1, the hot change values of candidate hot items are very low, resulting in the lowest final evaluation. Despite that the hot change score of the popularity method is relatively high, the spearman rank correlation coefficient of hot change is very low, leading to a low final evaluation. The ADHV and the Bayesian algorithm give a more consistent ranking trend of the candidate hot items within the time window and are more robust.

Table 5. Hot change values for different hot items recommendation on Sept. 23rd.

ADHV	Grapefruit	Cantaloupe	Leek	Corn	Beef offal	Strawberry	Tomato	Cherry	Seafood	Pineapple
Ranks on Sept. 23rd	1	2	3	4	5	6	7	8	9	10
Ranks on Sept. 25th	4	6	3	2	1	15	5	13	14	19
Hot change value	0.047	0.009	0.167	0.220	0.196	0.000	0.126	0.001	0.001	0.000
Hot change value order	5	6	3	1	2	9	4	7	8	10
Bayesian	**Shrimp**	**Guava**	**Grapefruit**	**Kiwi**	**Mooncake**	**Chicken**	**Beef**	**Prune**	**Crab**	**Matsutake**
Ranks on Sept. 23rd	1	2	3	4	5	6	7	8	9	10
Ranks on Sept. 25th	6	3	4	2	1	5	16	14	19	12
Hot change value	0.007	0.134	0.090	0.220	0.196	0.122	0.000	0.000	0.000	0.012
Hot change value order	7	3	5	1	2	4	9	8	10	6
Newton	**Grapefruit**	**Goose**	**Beef steak**	**Passion fruit**	**Matsutake**	**Gooseberry**	**Blueberry**	**Orange**	**Persimmon**	**Lobster**
Ranks on Sept. 23rd	1	2	3	4	5	6	6	6	6	10
Ranks on Sept. 25th	5	11	2	15	17	19	21	11	117	54
Hot change value	0.018	0.000	0.244	0.000	0.000	0.000	0.000	0.001	0.000	0.000
Hot change value order	2	4	1	5	6	7	8	3	10	9
Popularity	**Seafood**	**Pork**	**Mooncake**	**Apple**	**Fish**	**Grape**	**Beef**	**Chicken**	**Crab**	**Kiwi**
Ranks on Sept. 23rd	1	2	3	4	5	6	7	8	9	10
Ranks on Sept. 25th	2	5	1	3	6	4	8	9	7	10
Hot change value	0.269	0.024	0.294	0.183	0.054	0.147	0.038	0.034	0.098	0.050
Hot change value order	2	10	1	3	6	4	8	9	5	7

Table 6. HWE metrics for different hot items recommendation algorithms.

Ranking algorithm	Spearman rank correlation coefficient	HWE
ADHV	0.475	0.364
Bayesian	0.370	0.289
Newton	0.685	0.180
Popularity	0.235	0.280

6   Conclusions

To addressing the cold start problem in the express recommendation field, this paper proposes the ADHV algorithm by combining the concept of "hotness" with Bayesian thinking. From the use of the priori information of candidate items with the current popularity as an adjustment factor, the historical hot value of each candidate item is corrected, thereby accurately indicating the change of candidate items' hotness over time. This algorithm not only takes into account the sample size its change over time, but also combines the global sample information to give a reasonable rule for calculating the base hot value and hot weight factor. Moreover, the ADHV does not need to restrict the number of votes made by users, and it can also give a reasonable hot value for candidate items with decreased votes. Thus solving the issue of hot long-tail items not being recognized, and obtaining a more reasonable and accurate recommendation.

In addition, this paper also proposes an evaluation metric HWE for hot items recommendation algorithms. The evaluation combines the hot information with the idea of Newton's law of Cooling to give the hot change value of candidate items. And according to Spearman's correlation coefficient, the HWE of each recommended word is obtained. Experimental studies have shown that using HWE metric can effectively and objectively evaluate various hot ranking recommendation algorithms, avoiding subjective judgments.

References

1. Abdollahpouri, H., Mansoury, M., Burke, R., Mobasher, B.: The Unfairness of Popularity Bias in Recommendation (2019)
2. Aggarwal, C.: Content-based recommender systems. 139–166 (2016)
3. Bun, K., Ishizuka, M.: Topic extraction from news archive using TF*PDF algorithm. 73–82 (2003)
4. Burke, R.: Hybrid recommender systems: survey and experiments. User modeling and user-adapted interaction **12**, November 2002
5. Cao, L.: Coupling Learning of Complex Interactions (2020)
6. Cataldi, M., Di Caro, L., Schifanella, C.: Emerging topic detection on twitter based on temporal and social terms evaluation, July 2010

7. Chen, S.-H., Sou, S.-I., Hsieh, H.-P.: Top-N music recommendation framework for precision and novelty under diversity group size and similarity. J. Intell. Inform. Syst. **62**, 1–26, July 2023
8. Esmeli, R., Bader-El-Den, M., Abdullahi, H.: Session similarity based approach for alleviating cold-start session problem in e-commerce for Top-N recommendations, pp. 173–180 (2020)
9. Herlocker, J., Konstan, J., AlBorchers, Riedl, J.: An algorithmic framework for performing collaborative filtering. ACM SIGIR Forum **51**, 227–234, August 2017
10. Kuan-Yu, C., Luesukprasert, L., Chou, S.-C.: Hot topic extraction based on timeline analysis and multidimensional sentence modeling. IEEE Trans. Knowl. Data Eng. **19**, 1016–1025, September 2007
11. Lee, D., Hosanagar, K.: Impact of recommender systems on sales volume and diversity, January 2014
12. Liao, H., Mariani, M.S., Medo, M., Zhang, Y.-C., Zhou, M.Y.: Ranking in evolving complex networks. Phys. Rep. **689**, April 2017
13. Liu, N., Meng, X., Liu, C., Yang, Q.: Wisdom of the better few: cold start recommendation via representative based rating elicitation. In: RecSys 2011 Proceedings of the 5th ACM Conference on Recommender Systems, pp. 37–44 (2011)
14. Liu, Z., Fang, Y., Min, W.: Mitigating popularity bias for users and items with fairness-centric adaptive recommendation. ACM Trans.Inform. Syst. **3**(2023), 41 (2023)
15. Lu, X., Wu, J., Yuan, J.: Optimizing reciprocal rank with Bayesian average for improved next item recommendation, pp. 2236–2240 (2023)
16. Park, Y.-J., Tuzhilin, A.: The long tail of recommender systems and how to leverage it. In: RecSys 2008: Proceedings of the 2008 ACM Conference on Recommender Systems, pp. 11–18 (2008)
17. Ruan, Y.: Ranking algorithm based on user votes 2012. https://www.cnblogs.com/haore147/p/4986749.html
18. Schein, A., Popescul, A., Ungar, L., Pennock, D.: Methods and metrics for cold-start recommendations. In: SIGIR Forum (ACM Special Interest Group on Information Retrieval), pp. 253–260 (2002)
19. Son, L.: Dealing with the new user cold-start problem in recommender systems: a comparative review. Inform. Syst. **58,** December 2014
20. Steck, H.: Item popularity and recommendation accuracy, pp. 125–132 (2011)
21. Tian, D., Liu, Y., Wang, Y.: Literature measurement analysis of hot spot analysis articles——an example of word frequency analysis. Inform. Sci. **35**(8), 6 (2017)
22. Vojnovic, M., Cruise, J., Gunawardena, D., Marbach, P.: Ranking and suggesting popular items. IEEE Trans. Knowl. Data Eng. **21**, 1133–1146, September 2009
23. Wang, S., Wang, Y., Sheng, Q., Orgun, M., Cao, L., Lian, D.: A survey on session-based recommender systems, December 2020
24. Wu, C., Yan, M.: Session-aware information embedding for e-commerce product recommendation, pp. 2379–2382 (2017)
25. Zhang, M.: Research on Hot Topic Detection Methods for Microblog. Ph. D. Dissertation. Beijing Jiaotong University (2018)
26. Zhu, Z., He, Y., Zhao, X., , J.: Popularity bias in dynamic recommendation, pp. 2439–2449 (2021)

Retrieval-Augmented Generation Architecture Framework: Harnessing the Power of RAG

Richard Shan[(✉)] and Tony Shan

Computing Technology Solutions Inc., Charlotte, NC 28277, USA
m@richardshan.com

Abstract. This paper presents a comprehensive exploration of the Retrieval-Augmented Generation Architecture Framework (RAGAF), structured around seven key modules: Generator, Retriever, Orchestration, UI, Source, Evaluation, and Reranker (GROUSER). Each module plays a vital role in enabling dynamic information retrieval and contextually relevant response generation. The study discusses the enabling technologies that support these modules, including large language models, vector databases, knowledge bases, text processing, frontend technologies, orchestration tools, and hardware accelerators. Through a detailed case study in the domain of customer support, we demonstrate how the RAG architecture framework can enhance the efficiency and accuracy of customer interactions by generating accurate, context-aware responses while reducing human workload. The analysis highlights the strengths and challenges of RAG systems, offering insights into their optimization and deployment to achieve improved customer satisfaction and service quality in practical applications.

Keywords: Retrieval-Augmented Generation · RAG architecture · framework · natural language processing · generative models · large language models · text embedding · vector database · multimodal data integration · evaluation metrics

1 Introduction

The rapid advancement of artificial intelligence (AI) and natural language processing (NLP) has ushered in a new era of intelligent systems capable of understanding and generating human-like text. Among these advancements, Retrieval-Augmented Generation (RAG) has emerged as a powerful approach that combines the strengths of retrieval-based models and generative language models. Unlike traditional generative models that rely solely on pre-trained knowledge, RAG systems dynamically incorporate external information [1], enabling more accurate, relevant, and context-aware responses. RAG systems can be broadly categorized into Naive, Advanced, and Modular RAGs [2], each offering distinct strategies for text generation tasks such as dialogue response generation, machine translation, and other generative applications [3]. Evaluating RAG effectiveness is critical [4], with an emphasis on assessing retrieval quality [5], which can be enhanced through benchmark processes [6] and automated tools like RAGAS [7]. Advanced methods, such as retrieval fusion techniques [8], have been applied to improve RAG performance in NLP tasks. Recent innovations in RAG include the Forward-Looking Active

© The Author(s), under exclusive license to Springer Nature Switzerland AG 2025
R. Xu et al. (Eds.): ICCC 2024, LNCS 15426, pp. 88–104, 2025.
https://doi.org/10.1007/978-3-031-77954-1_6

RAG, which anticipates future content by predicting upcoming sentences [9], and the Unified Active Retrieval (UAR) [10], which optimizes retrieval timing through multi-faceted judgment criteria. Iterative retrieval-generation processes have also been shown to create a synergistic enhancement in RAG effectiveness [11]. Other developments, such as Corrective RAG, employ lightweight retrieval evaluators to refine outputs [12], while Graph RAG integrates graph structures to bolster both retrieval and generation [13]. Additionally, combining RAG with long-context large language models (LLMs) has demonstrated improved performance metrics like F1 scores [14], and approaches such as Chain-of-Note further enhance RAG robustness by managing complex dependencies [15].

While substantial progress has been made in Retrieval-Augmented Generation methodologies, there is still a significant need for a comprehensive analysis of architectural design principles, the interaction between modules, and the practical challenges of deploying and scaling RAG systems in real-world applications. A generic framework was presented with only retrievers and generators for surveying AI-generated content [16]. However, more nuanced approaches, like a block diagram emphasizing the use of text chunks, aim to eliminate inefficiencies, provide intermediate results for better system transparency, and enable two-way interaction with end users [17]. Some studies have developed specialized RAG frameworks tailored to specific domains. For example, a retrieval-augmented LLM was enhanced with a comprehensive ophthalmic dataset (CODE), comprising over 30,000 pieces of ophthalmic knowledge, to improve clinical decision-making [18]. Another architecture, Prof. Leodar, was designed as a custom GenAI chatbot to provide personalized learning support for students, with a detailed workflow outlining its functionality [19]. In the medical field, a flowchart-based RAG architecture was proposed for clinical note-based question answering [20], while a highly extensible RAG architecture was utilized for clinical decision support in bipolar depression [21]. Further advancements include a system sequence diagram illustrating the process flow in a hybrid context RAG [22], and a refined retrieval performance achieved by tuning the embedding retrieval module through backpropagation of errors across combined retrieval and generation tasks, such as question answering and citation suggestion [23]. In addition, innovative approaches like a code-free RAG architecture were applied to ophthalmology [24], and the GenFlowchart framework utilized RAG to enhance the parsing and interpretation of complex flowcharts [25].

It is important to provide a comprehensive exploration of the RAG architecture framework, its technical components, and the enabling technologies that underpin it. This study aims to address the gaps by presenting an in-depth analysis of the RAG framework's architecture, identifying its key components, and discussing the technologies and techniques that support these components. Additionally, the paper will explore the strengths and limitations of the enabling technologies. Through a case study, we will highlight successful implementations of RAG systems, providing insights into their applications, benefits, and challenges.

The key contributions of this paper are threefold:

- A detailed breakdown of the RAG architecture and its core components, offering a clear understanding of how retrieval and generation processes are integrated to achieve superior performance.

- An analysis of the enabling technologies and their pros and cons, providing guidance for researchers and practitioners on selecting appropriate tools and frameworks for developing RAG systems.
- A case study that demonstrates the practical applications of RAG architecture framework in a specific domain, highlighting best practices, outcomes, and lessons learned.

By shedding light on these aspects, this paper aims to serve as a foundational resource for academics, researchers, and industry professionals interested in the architecture and implementation of RAG systems. Furthermore, it seeks to encourage future research in optimizing RAG architectures and expanding their applications to new and emerging fields.

2   Retrieval-Augmented Generation Architecture Framework

The RAG Architecture Framework (RAGAF) is designed to combine the strengths of retrieval-based methods and generative models, creating a robust system capable of producing accurate, contextually grounded responses. The architecture of a RAG framework consists of seven core components: Generator, Retriever, Orchestration, UI, Source, Evaluation, and Reranker (GROUSER), illustrated in Fig. 1. Each of these components plays a distinct yet interconnected role in enhancing the overall performance of the system.

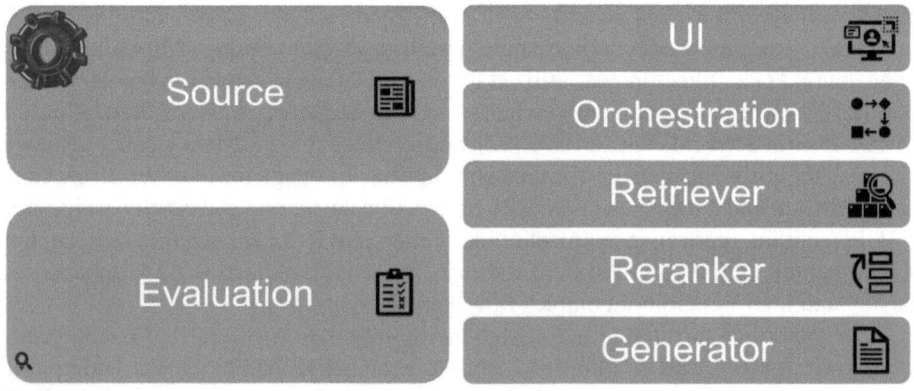

Fig. 1. RAG Architecture Framework

2.1   Source Module

The first crucial component in a RAG system is the Source Module for data processing and preprocessing pipeline. Data preprocessing is essential to prepare raw data for the retriever and generator modules, ensuring that the information is relevant, structured, and in a format suitable for retrieval and generation tasks.

There are several key steps in data processing and preprocessing:

- Data Cleaning: Involves removing noise, correcting errors, and standardizing formats within the data. This step ensures the quality and consistency of the input data, which is critical for both retrieval and generation.
- Tokenization: Splits the text into tokens (words or subwords) that can be processed by language models. Tokenization is vital for converting text into a format that embedding methods can handle efficiently.
- Normalization: Converts text to a uniform format (e.g., lowercasing, stemming, or lemmatization) to reduce variability and improve the performance of retrieval algorithms, especially in cases where exact matches are required.
- Chunking: Divides large documents into smaller, manageable chunks using text splitters. This step is crucial for ensuring that the retriever can efficiently search for relevant information and that the generator can produce contextually accurate responses.
- Embedding Generation: Computes embeddings for text chunks using pre-trained models (e.g., BERT, Sentence-BERT). These embeddings are then indexed in vector databases for efficient similarity search.

The primary challenges in data processing include:

- Scalability: Processing large volumes of data in real-time can be computationally expensive, requiring optimized pipelines and hardware acceleration.
- Data Quality and Bias: Poor quality data can degrade the performance of both retrieval and generation. Additionally, biases in the data can lead to biased outputs, necessitating careful data curation and filtering.

2.2 UI Module

The User interface (UI) Module is a crucial component for building a user-friendly web interface for interacting with a RAG system. This module is responsible for presenting the system's functionalities to end users in an accessible and intuitive way, allowing them to input queries, receive results, and visualize the retrieval and generation process. Tools like Streamlit provide a powerful and flexible framework for rapidly developing web applications that showcase RAG capabilities.

The key features of the UI module are:

- Interactive Query Interface: Provides a streamlined and responsive input area where users can enter queries or requests. This interface is designed to handle various input types, such as text, voice, or file uploads, and dynamically update as users interact with the system.
- Result Display and Visualization: Presents the retrieved documents and generated outputs in an organized, easy-to-read format. The UI may include features such as highlighting relevant information, displaying confidence scores, or providing side-by-side comparisons of different responses to enhance user understanding.
- Real-time Feedback Loop: Enables users to provide feedback on the quality of the results. This feedback can be integrated into the RAG system to refine future outputs, enhancing the overall adaptability and performance of the system.

The predominant UI development frameworks include:

- Streamlit: A popular open-source framework specifically designed for creating machine learning and data science web applications. Streamlit enables rapid development and deployment of RAG web interfaces with minimal coding, allowing developers to focus on building functional and visually appealing applications.
- Dash: A Python framework for building analytical web applications, suitable for more complex interfaces that require advanced visualization capabilities or interactive features beyond basic RAG functionality.
- Gradio: Another user-friendly interface builder for machine learning applications, offering easy integration with RAG models to create interactive demos or prototypes that showcase system capabilities.

The customization and extension capabilities comprise:

- Custom Widgets and Controls: Allows the development of bespoke widgets, sliders, and controls to enhance user interaction, such as adjusting retrieval parameters, filtering results, or selecting different generation models.
- Visualization Tools: Integrates with data visualization libraries like Plotly or Matplotlib to provide dynamic visualizations of retrieval paths, confidence levels, or other performance metrics, improving transparency and user engagement.

The challenges in UI development entail:

- User Experience Optimization: Ensuring the interface is intuitive and accessible to users with varying levels of technical expertise, while also providing sufficient functionality for advanced users.
- Performance and Responsiveness: Maintaining real-time responsiveness and performance of the UI, especially when handling complex queries or large volumes of data, requires careful optimization and efficient design.
- Security and Privacy Considerations: Protecting user data and maintaining secure communication channels between the UI and backend components, especially when deploying RAG systems that handle sensitive or confidential information.

2.3 Orchestration Module

The Orchestration Module is essential for coordinating the multiple components of a RAG system, managing the flow of data, and optimizing the overall performance from data ingestion to final output. This module ensures that each component—retriever, reranker, generator, and UI—functions cohesively and efficiently, both in research settings and in production environments. By leveraging orchestration frameworks like RAGNA, the Orchestration Module provides a scalable, flexible, and customizable infrastructure for deploying RAG systems.

The key features of orchestration frameworks consist of:

- Component Management: Allows dynamic management of individual RAG components, such as retrievers and generators, enabling seamless integration, version control, and updates without disrupting the entire system. This modular approach enhances flexibility and adaptability across different tasks and domains.

- Pipeline Optimization: Automatically optimizes the end-to-end RAG pipeline by managing task dependencies, allocating computational resources, and reducing bottlenecks. This ensures efficient data flow and minimizes latency, especially critical in real-time applications.
- Monitoring and Logging: Provides tools for real-time monitoring and logging, enabling continuous performance evaluation, debugging, and fine-tuning. These tools allow for the detection of issues such as model drift, data inconsistencies, or latency spikes, facilitating rapid response and system optimization.

There are several orchestration strategies:

- Task Scheduling and Load Balancing: Uses advanced scheduling algorithms to allocate tasks across multiple resources, balancing load and minimizing execution time. This is particularly important in high-traffic environments or applications requiring low-latency responses.
- Dynamic Configuration and Scaling: Supports dynamic scaling of system components based on workload demands, allowing the RAG system to adjust resources in real-time, optimizing both performance and cost. This approach is crucial for production-level deployments where traffic and data volume can fluctuate significantly.
- Modular Architecture and Reusability: Facilitates the reuse of pre-configured modules and components across different projects or applications, promoting faster development and deployment cycles. Orchestration frameworks like RAGNA provide templates and pre-built configurations that speed up the integration of new components or data sources.

The challenges in orchestration embrace:

- Complexity in Integration: Managing the integration of multiple components, each potentially using different technologies or frameworks, can be challenging and requires robust interface management and API standardization.
- Scalability Across Heterogeneous Environments: Ensuring that the orchestration framework scales efficiently across diverse environments, from small-scale research setups to large-scale production systems, requires sophisticated infrastructure management and adaptability.
- Resource Optimization: Balancing computational resources across various components while maintaining optimal system performance can be difficult, particularly in resource-constrained or cost-sensitive scenarios.

2.4 Retriever Module

The Retriever is responsible for identifying and retrieving the most relevant information from an external knowledge source. It can be further categorized into two main types:

- Sparse Retrievers: These traditional methods rely on keyword matching and use sparse representations, such as TF-IDF (Term Frequency-Inverse Document Frequency) or BM25 (Best Matching 25). Sparse retrievers are highly interpretable and efficient for specific use cases where keyword-based retrieval is sufficient. However, they may struggle with semantic similarity and are less effective for complex or nuanced queries.

- Dense Retrievers: Dense retrievers leverage deep learning models, such as bi-encoders or dual encoders, to map queries and documents into a dense vector space, where similarity is measured using metrics like cosine similarity. Examples of dense retrieval models include DPR (Dense Passage Retrieval) and ColBERT (Contextualized Late Interaction over BERT). Dense retrievers like ANCE (Approximate Nearest Context Encoder) are capable of capturing semantic similarities and nuances but often require significant computational resources for training and inference.

The algorithms and technologies for retrieval also involve hybrid approaches that combines sparse and dense retrieval to leverage the advantages of both. The performance considerations and optimizations encompass:

- Trade-offs between accuracy and efficiency
- Indexing and storage strategies for large-scale retrieval
- Use of hardware accelerators (e.g., GPUs) for faster vector search operations
- Alternatively, a vector database can be used as a retriever

2.5   Generator Module

The Generator is responsible for synthesizing coherent and contextually relevant text based on the information retrieved by the retriever. This module typically uses large-scale pre-trained language models, such as GPT, BERT, or T5, which are fine-tuned to produce outputs grounded in the retrieved content.

There a few types of language models used:

- Auto-regressive models (e.g., GPT): Generate text one token at a time, using the previously generated tokens as context.
- Encoder-decoder models (e.g., T5, BART): Use an encoder to understand the input context and a decoder to generate the output, allowing for more flexible handling of input types and lengths.
- Bidirectional models (e.g., BERT): Used in contexts where understanding the entire input context is essential before generating the output.

The training methodologies and fine-tuning are:

- Supervised fine-tuning on domain-specific datasets
- Reinforcement learning from human feedback (RLHF) for aligning model outputs with user expectations.
- Techniques to reduce model hallucinations and improve coherence

The challenges in generation include:

- Hallucination: The tendency of models to produce plausible-sounding but factually incorrect information.
- Coherence and Fluency: Ensuring that generated text is logical, flows well, and maintains contextual relevance.
- Controllability: Ability to guide the model's output to adhere to specific styles, tones, or factual constraints.

2.6   Reranker Module

The Reranker Module is a crucial component in a RAG system, responsible for refining and prioritizing the retrieved documents or passages to enhance the relevance and quality of the generated output. After the retriever identifies a set of potentially relevant documents, the reranker module re-evaluates and reorders these documents based on a more nuanced understanding of their relevance to the query, thus improving the overall performance of the system.

There are several types of reranking models used:

- Cross-encoder Models (e.g., BERT Cross-encoder): Evaluate each query-document pair by jointly encoding them, allowing the model to capture fine-grained interactions between the query and the text. This method, while computationally expensive, often provides the highest accuracy in determining relevance.
- Bi-encoder Models (e.g., Dual Encoder): Independently encode the query and document into separate vectors, and then compute their similarity. Bi-encoders are more efficient than cross-encoders and can handle large-scale retrieval but may sacrifice some accuracy due to their less interactive nature.
- Hybrid Reranking Models: Combine both cross-encoder and bi-encoder approaches to balance accuracy and computational efficiency. Hybrid models may use a bi-encoder for initial filtering and a cross-encoder for final reranking, optimizing the performance-cost trade-off.

The training methodologies for reranking is composed of:

- Supervised Learning with Large Datasets: Involves training the reranker on large-scale annotated datasets where relevance labels are provided for query-document pairs. This method ensures the reranker learns to distinguish between highly relevant and less relevant documents.
- Contrastive Learning: Enhances the model's ability to differentiate between similar and dissimilar pairs by training it on contrastive loss, which encourages the model to bring relevant pairs closer in the embedding space and push irrelevant ones further apart.
- Domain-Specific Fine-Tuning: Fine-tuning the reranker on domain-specific data to better capture the nuances and contextual relevance specific to particular applications (e.g., legal documents, medical literature).

The challenges in reranking comprise:

- Computational Complexity: Cross-encoders, which provide higher accuracy, are computationally intensive, requiring significant resources, especially for large-scale retrieval tasks.
- Balancing Precision and Recall: Ensuring that the reranker maintains a balance between precision (retrieving only the most relevant documents) and recall (retrieving all relevant documents) can be challenging, particularly in domains with vast amounts of data.
- Adaptability to Domain Changes: The reranker needs to remain effective across different domains and contexts, which may require continuous retraining or fine-tuning to handle evolving data distributions and query types.

2.7   Evaluation Module

The Evaluation Module is essential for assessing the performance, reliability, and quality of a RAG system. This module is responsible for measuring the effectiveness of both retrieval and generation components, ensuring that the system meets its intended objectives and performs optimally across different use cases. Evaluation is conducted using a combination of automated metrics, human assessments, and domain-specific benchmarks to provide a comprehensive understanding of the system's capabilities and limitations.

There are multiple types of evaluation metrics used:

- Retrieval Metrics:

o Precision@K: Measures the proportion of relevant documents among the top K results, indicating how accurately the retriever identifies the most pertinent information.
o Recall@K: Evaluates the proportion of all relevant documents retrieved within the top K results, ensuring that the system captures as much useful information as possible.
o Mean Reciprocal Rank (MRR): Calculates the average of reciprocal ranks of relevant documents, reflecting the effectiveness of the retriever in positioning useful information at the top.

- Generation Metrics:

o BLEU and ROUGE: Standard metrics for comparing generated text with reference texts, measuring n-gram overlap and ensuring outputs are coherent and contextually appropriate.
o METEOR: A metric that aligns generated outputs with reference texts using synonyms, paraphrases, and stemmed variations, offering a more nuanced assessment of text quality.
o Fact-Consistency Scores (e.g., FactCC, QAGS): Evaluate the factual accuracy of generated content, ensuring that outputs are consistent with the retrieved information.

The evaluation methodologies and techniques are comprised of:

- Automated Evaluation: Utilizes pre-defined metrics to provide a quantitative assessment of system performance, facilitating rapid and repeatable evaluations during development and deployment.
- Human Evaluation: Involves human judges to assess outputs for relevance, fluency, factuality, and coherence, capturing qualitative aspects that automated metrics may miss.
- Domain-Specific Benchmarks: Employs datasets like Natural Questions (NQ), MS MARCO, and SQuAD to evaluate system performance in specific contexts, ensuring the model meets domain-specific requirements.

The challenges in evaluation entail:

- Metric Limitations: Automated metrics like BLEU and ROUGE often fail to capture the full range of quality dimensions, necessitating the use of human evaluation to understand system performance comprehensively.

- Human Subjectivity: Human evaluation is prone to subjectivity and variability, requiring well-defined guidelines and multiple raters to ensure consistency and reliability.
- Dynamic Evaluation Needs: As RAG systems are applied across various domains, the evaluation module must adapt to different contexts and evolving requirements, requiring continuous updates to metrics and benchmarks.

2.8 Interactions Between Components

The components of the RAG architecture collaborate in a tightly integrated workflow to produce high-quality, contextually relevant outputs. Source serves as the repository of data from which the retriever pulls relevant information, encompassing various types such as text, images, or multimodal datasets. The UI Module facilitates user interaction with the system by providing a web-based interface for inputting queries, visualizing retrieval processes, and presenting the generated responses, while also capturing user feedback. Subsequently, the Orchestration Module manages and coordinates the interactions between all these components, optimizing task allocation, managing dependencies, and scaling resources to ensure seamless and efficient operation from data ingestion to output generation. Afterwards, the Retriever identifies the most relevant documents or passages from the Source, providing initial candidates that form the basis of the generated response. Then the Reranker re-evaluates and reorders the retrieved documents, ensuring that the most relevant and high-quality information is prioritized before passing it on. And the Generator synthesizes coherent and contextually informed responses based on the refined set of retrieved content provided by the reranker, creating outputs that are tailored to the query or user input. Finally, the Evaluation Module continuously monitors the performance of the RAG system, applying a mix of automated metrics and human feedback to assess the quality and effectiveness of outputs and inform ongoing adjustments and improvements.

This tightly coupled interaction among all components enables the RAG system to dynamically incorporate new data, refine outputs, and adapt to changing requirements, resulting in responses that are more accurate, relevant, and context-aware than those produced by traditional generative models alone.

3 Enabling Technologies

The successful deployment of RAG systems relies on a robust combination of advanced technologies that underpin each component of the architecture. These enabling technologies provide the computational power, storage solutions, optimization capabilities, and integration frameworks required to support dynamic retrieval, sophisticated generation, and seamless user interaction.

3.1 UI Tools

UI tools like Chainlit and Streamlit are essential for developing web applications that allow end-users to interact with RAG systems.

- Chainlit: Provides an environment tailored for conversational AI interfaces, allowing developers to create custom user experiences that can interact with the RAG system's back-end components.
- Streamlit: An open-source framework for quickly building and deploying web-based applications, Streamlit supports interactive features such as sliders, buttons, and dynamic visualizations, making it ideal for prototyping and deploying RAG user interfaces.

These tools enable rapid development, iterative testing, and deployment of user-friendly interfaces, enhancing the accessibility and usability of RAG systems.

3.2 Orchestration Technologies

Orchestration technologies are vital for managing the complex interactions between components in a RAG system. They facilitate seamless communication, data flow, and integration, enabling efficient coordination of retrieval, generation, and user interaction processes.

- LangChain: An open-source framework for building applications around large language models, allowing developers to chain together components such as retrievers, generators, and integrators in a flexible manner. It simplifies component integration, prompt management, and memory handling, significantly reducing development time and complexity.
- LlamaIndex: Focuses on efficient indexing and querying between language models and external data sources, optimizing retrieval processes to access the most relevant information quickly. It supports customizable pipelines, query optimization, and multiple data formats, enhancing the performance and scalability of RAG systems.

Both frameworks are instrumental in creating flexible, scalable RAG applications, providing robust tools for managing the dynamic and complex interactions of different components.

3.3 Text Processing

Efficient text processing is essential for optimizing both retrieval and generation in RAG architectures. Text splitters and embedding methods are key components that help structure and represent text for effective information retrieval and response generation.

- Text Splitters: Divide large documents into smaller, contextually coherent chunks, improving retrieval efficiency and ensuring that language models operate on relevant text segments. Granularity, context preservation, and domain-specific rules are critical considerations in text splitting strategies.

- Embedding Methods: Transform text into numerical vectors, enabling similarity searches and relevance scoring. Contextual word embeddings (e.g., BERT, RoBERTa), sentence embeddings (e.g., Sentence-BERT), and dense passage embeddings (e.g., DPR, ColBERT) are commonly used to enhance retrieval accuracy and performance.

These methods are fundamental to the operation of RAG systems, allowing for fast similarity searches and grounded content generation.

3.4 Vector Database

Vector databases are pivotal in the retrieval component of RAG systems. They store documents or passages in vectorized form and utilize efficient similarity search algorithms to locate the most relevant information for a given query.

- FAISS (Facebook AI Similarity Search): An open-source library optimized for performance and scalability, supporting large-scale similarity search and clustering of dense vectors.
- Pinecone: A managed vector database offering high-speed similarity search and retrieval, supporting hybrid retrieval methods and real-time updates for production environments.
- Elasticsearch with Vector Search: Extends the traditional Elasticsearch engine to support dense vector search, enabling seamless integration for users familiar with text-based search.

These engines enable scalable and accurate retrieval but demand significant memory and storage resources and require careful configuration to handle large datasets effectively.

3.5 Knowledge Bases and Graph Databases

Knowledge bases and graph databases provide structured, domain-specific information that enhances both retrieval and generation in RAG systems.

- Wikidata and ConceptNet: Open knowledge bases offering structured data to ground generated content in factual information, crucial for domain-specific applications like medical or legal information retrieval.
- Neo4j and Amazon Neptune: Graph databases that represent data as nodes and edges, allowing complex relationship-based queries suitable for applications requiring deep entity understanding, such as personalized recommendations.

While these resources offer high accuracy and interpretability, maintaining them can be challenging, particularly in rapidly evolving domains.

3.6   Large Language Models and Foundational Models

Large language models such as GPT, BERT, and T5 form the core of the generation component in RAG systems. These models are pre-trained on massive datasets to produce fluent, contextually appropriate responses based on dynamically retrieved information.

- GPT (Generative Pre-trained Transformer): An auto-regressive model that generates text by predicting the next word in a sequence, ideal for open-ended text generation tasks. GPT is widely adopted in RAG systems for its ability to produce coherent and contextually relevant responses.
- BERT (Bidirectional Encoder Representations from Transformers): A bidirectional model that understands the semantics of input text by considering context from both directions. BERT is often used in retrieval tasks to improve the quality and relevance of retrieved documents.
- T5 (Text-to-Text Transfer Transformer): An encoder-decoder model that frames all NLP tasks as text-to-text problems, making it versatile for both retrieval and generation tasks. Its flexibility is particularly advantageous in RAG systems that require complex understanding and contextual generation capabilities.

These models are fundamental to generating high-quality outputs but pose challenges such as high computational costs, latency, and the need for domain-specific fine-tuning to mitigate issues like hallucination and irrelevance.

3.7   Hardware Accelerators

Hardware accelerators, such as GPUs (Graphics Processing Units), TPUs (Tensor Processing Units), and FPGAs (Field-Programmable Gate Arrays), are crucial for enhancing the speed and scalability of RAG systems.

- GPUs: Optimize parallel processing, making them ideal for large-scale neural network computations, balancing performance and flexibility across diverse AI workloads.
- TPUs: Specialized for deep learning workloads, providing high performance for training and inference in large-scale RAG applications.
- FPGAs: Offer customizable hardware acceleration for specific tasks like search and retrieval, providing flexibility and efficiency but requiring more development effort.

While these accelerators significantly boost performance, they involve trade-offs in cost, power consumption, and deployment complexity, necessitating careful selection based on application requirements.

3.8   Comparative Analysis

The comparison of the key enabling technologies is highlighted in Fig. 2, which provides a comprehensive evaluation of the building blocks for RAG systems, contrasting their pros and cons in terms of scalability, performance, cost-efficiency, and ease of integration. It helps stakeholders select the most suitable tools and approaches for specific applications.

Technology	Pros	Cons
Large Language Models	High-quality text generation; adaptability to various tasks	High computational cost; potential for hallucination; fine-tuning needed
Vector Databases	Fast and accurate retrieval; scalable to large datasets	High memory/storage requirements; difficulty in setup and maintenance
Knowledge Bases/Graph Databases	Structured and factual grounding; high accuracy and interpretability	Skillset challenges; limited flexibility in dynamic domains
Hardware Accelerators	Enhanced performance; scalability; optimized for ML workloads	High cost; power consumption; deployment complexity; vendor lock-in
Orchestration Technologies	Facilitate integration; improve modularity and flexibility	Architectural complexity; may require customization to specific cases
UI Tools	Rapid development and deployment; enhance accessibility	Limited to the capabilities of the UI framework: scalability challenges

Fig. 2. Pros and Cons of Enabling Technologies

4   Implementation

To illustrate the practical applications and benefits of the RAGAF, we delve into a case study, which demonstrates how RAG systems have been implemented to solve real-world problems, the outcomes achieved, the challenges faced during implementation, and the lessons learned.

Customer support services require efficient handling of a large number of queries, many of which are repetitive or require access to vast knowledge bases. Traditional rule-based chatbots often fail to provide satisfactory responses due to their limited understanding and inability to access dynamic, real-time information. A RAG system was deployed to enhance customer support by generating accurate, context-aware responses, reducing the workload on human agents.

A dense retriever model was trained on a dataset containing FAQs, user manuals, product documentation, and historical customer service transcripts. The retriever was optimized to fetch the most relevant passages based on customer queries. An encoder-decoder model was fine-tuned to generate responses that are coherent, contextually appropriate, and aligned with the brand's tone. The model was trained on customer interaction datasets to capture the nuances of customer service conversations.

A graph database (Neo4j) was integrated to provide structured information, such as troubleshooting steps or policy details, ensuring that responses were both accurate and actionable. LlamaIndex was used to orchestrate the queries to the large and heterogeneous data sources involved, optimizing response times and ensuring high relevance.

The RAG system improved first-contact resolution rates and customer satisfaction by providing accurate and contextually relevant responses. It also enabled human agents to focus on more complex queries, improving overall service efficiency. The integration of a graph database allowed for more structured and detailed responses, particularly for complex queries. Continuous monitoring and retraining of the retrieval model were necessary to handle evolving product information and customer concerns.

In addition, RAGAF has been successfully employed in other domains, such as applications in healthcare for personalized treatment and applications in education for adaptive learning. In some scenarios, the overall RAG architecture was streamlined in the simplified implementation to reduce the complexity, particularly for the prototype and MVP. For example, the Reranker module was not utilized, with the additional tuning and optimization in the Retriever module.

5 Conclusion

Retrieval-Augmented Generation represents a significant advancement in the field of artificial intelligence, combining the strengths of retrieval-based methods with generative models to create systems capable of producing contextually relevant and accurate outputs. This paper has provided an in-depth exploration of the RAG architecture framework, covering its key components, enabling technologies, and practical applications across various domains.

RAG systems have demonstrated their potential in domains like healthcare, education, and customer support, where they have significantly enhanced decision-making, personalized services, and efficiency. By dynamically retrieving relevant information and grounding generated outputs in this context, RAG systems can address many of the limitations of standalone generative models, such as hallucinations and the lack of up-to-date knowledge. Through the use of orchestration tools like LangChain and LlamaIndex, and techniques such as text splitting and advanced embedding methods, RAG architectures have become more flexible, scalable, and effective in handling complex information retrieval and generation tasks.

However, RAG systems still face several challenges, including latency, scalability, data quality, and model hallucination, which require further research and innovation. Future directions include developing adaptive and continual learning models, integrating multimodal data, improving pipeline optimization, and enhancing security and privacy measures. New domains such as legal research, financial services, scientific discovery, and urban planning present promising opportunities for expanding the application of RAG systems.

To ensure the continued advancement and successful deployment of RAG systems, a comprehensive evaluation strategy that includes both standard metrics and domain-specific techniques is essential. This approach will help identify the strengths and weaknesses of RAG systems, guiding further development efforts and ensuring they meet the unique needs of various industries.

- Architecture and Components: RAG systems combine retrieval and generation in a unified framework, using modules such as retrievers, generators, and integrators to create contextually grounded outputs.
- Enabling Technologies: Technologies like large language models, Vector databases, knowledge bases, and hardware accelerators support the performance and scalability of RAG systems, while orchestration tools optimize their operation.

- Practical Applications: RAG systems have been successfully implemented in healthcare, education, and customer support, demonstrating their ability to deliver personalized and context-aware information.
- Evaluation and Benchmarking: A combination of automated metrics, human evaluations, and domain-specific benchmarks is necessary for accurately assessing the performance and reliability of RAG systems.
- Challenges and Future Directions: Addressing issues like latency, hallucination, and bias, and exploring new areas like adaptive learning and multimodal integration, will drive future improvements in RAG systems.

The development and deployment of RAG systems are at an exciting juncture, with substantial opportunities for further research and innovation. By addressing current challenges and exploring new applications, RAG systems are poised to become a critical component of intelligent systems in the future. This study serves as a foundational resource for academics, researchers, and industry professionals interested in understanding and leveraging the potential of RAG architectures to transform their fields.

References

1. Lewis, P., et al.: Retrieval-augmented generation for knowledge-intensive NLP tasks. Adv. Neural. Inf. Process. Syst. **33**, 9459–9474 (2020)
2. Gao, Y., et al.: Retrieval-augmented generation for large language models: a survey. arXiv: 2312.10997 (2023)
3. Li, H., Su, Y., Cai, D., Wang, Y., Liu, L.: A survey on retrieval-augmented text generation. arXiv:2202.01110 (2022)
4. Yu, H., Gan, A., Zhang, K., Tong, S., Liu, Q., Liu, Z.: Evaluation of Retrieval-Augmented Generation: a Survey. arXiv:2405.07437 (2024)
5. Salemi, A., Zamani, H.: Evaluating retrieval quality in retrieval-augmented generation. In: Proceedings of the 47th International ACM SIGIR Conference on Research and Development in Information Retrieval, pp. 2395–2400 (2024). ISBN: 979-8-4007-0431-4
6. Chen, J., Lin, H., Han, X., Sun, L.: Benchmarking large language models in retrieval-augmented generation. In: Proceedings of the AAAI Conference on Artificial Intelligence, vol. 38, no. 16, 17754-17762 (2024)
7. Es, S., James, J., Espinosa-Anke, L., Schockaert, S.: Ragas: automated evaluation of retrieval augmented generation. arXiv:2309.15217 (2023)
8. Wu, S., et al.: Retrieval-Augmented Generation for Natural Language Processing: A Survey. arXiv:2407.13193 (2024)
9. Jiang, Z., et al.: Active retrieval augmented generation. arXiv:2305.06983 (2023)
10. Cheng, Q., et al.: Unified Active Retrieval for Retrieval Augmented Generation. arXiv:2406. 12534 (2024)
11. Shao, Z., Gong, Y., Shen, Y., Huang, M., Duan, N., Chen, W.: Enhancing retrieval-augmented large language models with iterative retrieval-generation synergy. arXiv:2305.15294 (2023)
12. Yan, S.Q., Gu, J.C., Zhu, Y., Ling, Z.H.: Corrective retrieval augmented generation. arXiv: 2401.15884 (2024)
13. Hu, Y., Lei, Z., Zhang, Z., Pan, B., Ling, C., Zhao, L.: GRAG: Graph Retrieval-Augmented Generation. arXiv:2405.16506 (2024)
14. Jiang, Z., Ma, X., Chen, W.: Longrag: Enhancing retrieval-augmented generation with long-context LLMs. arXiv:2406.15319 (2024)

15. Yu, W., Zhang, H., Pan, X., Ma, K., Wang, H., Yu, D.: Chain-of-note: enhancing robustness in retrieval-augmented language models. arXiv:2311.09210 (2023)
16. Zhao, P., et al.: Retrieval-augmented generation for AI-generated content: a survey. arXiv: 2402.19473 (2024)
17. Rakotoson, L., Massip, S., Laleye, F.A.: Science Checker Reloaded: A Bidirectional Paradigm for Transparency and Logical Reasoning. arXiv:2402.13897 (2024)
18. Luo, M. J., et al.: Development and evaluation of a retrieval-augmented large language model framework for ophthalmology. JAMA Ophthalmol. **142**(9), 798–805, 1 September 2024. https://doi.org/10.1001/jamaophthalmol.2024.2513
19. Thway, M., Recatala-Gomez, J., Lim, F.S., Hippalgaonkar, K., Ng, L.W.: Harnessing GenAI for Higher Education: a Study of a Retrieval Augmented Generation Chatbot's Impact on Human Learning. arXiv:2406.07796 (2024)
20. Unlu, O., et al.: Retrieval augmented generation enabled generative pre-trained transformer 4 (GPT-4) performance for clinical trial screening. medRxiv PMC10871450 (2024). https://doi.org/10.1101/2024.02.08.24302376
21. Perlis, R.H., Goldberg, J.F., Ostacher, M.J., Schneck, C.D.: Clinical decision support for bipolar depression using large language models. Neuropsychopharmacol. **49**(9),1412–1416, August 2024. https://doi.org/10.1038/s41386-024-01841-2
22. Edwards, C.: Hybrid Context Retrieval Augmented Generation Pipeline: LLM-Augmented Knowledge Graphs and Vector Database for Accreditation Reporting Assistance. arXiv:2405.15436 (2024)
23. Muther, R., Smith, D.: Citations as Queries: Source Attribution Using Language Models as Rerankers. arXiv:2306.17322 (2023)
24. Aykut, A., Sezenoz, A.S.: Exploring the potential of code-free custom GPTs in ophthalmology: an early analysis of GPT store and user-creator guidance. Ophthalmol. Therapy, 1–17 (2024)
25. Arbaz, A., Fan, H., Ding, J., Qiu, M., Feng, Y.: *GenFlowchart*: parsing and understanding flowchart using generative AI. In: Cao, C., Chen, H., Zhao, L., Arshad, J., Asyhari, T., Wang, Y. (eds.) Knowledge Science, Engineering and Management. KSEM 2024. Lecture Notes in Computer Science(), vol. 14884. Springer, Singapore (2024). https://doi.org/10.1007/978-981-97-5492-2_8

Short Paper Track

Application and Optimization of Multi-agent Reinforcement Learning in Collaborative Decision-Making

Qi Sun$^{(\boxtimes)}$ 🆔, Zhihao Chen 🆔, and Han Liu 🆔

College of Computer Science and Software Engineering, Hohai University, Nanjing, China
221307050009@hhu.edu.cn

Abstract. With the rapid development of intelligent systems, Multi-Agent Systems (MAS) have shown unique advantages in solving complex decision-making problems. Particularly in the field of Multi-Agent Reinforcement Learning (MARL), Multiple agents can decompose complex tasks, process information and make decisions in parallel, share experiences, accelerate the learning process, and significantly improve decision quality and efficiency. This paper explores the theoretical underpinnings of MARL and its application to collaborative decision-making and analyzes practical cases in areas such as transportation system management, automated manufacturing, and smart grids. Additionally, it addresses challenges in strategy coordination, handling dynamic environments, and improving learning efficiency. This paper proposes several optimization strategies and introduces reservoir group optimization experiments. By comparing with single-agent algorithms, it verifies that multi-agent systems can coordinate multiple reservoirs, enhance convergence speed, and achieve higher power generation efficiency, demonstrating better practical application prospects. Furthermore, the future trends of MARL, including technological advancements, potential applications, and challenges, are discussed.

Keywords: Multi-agent systems · Reinforcement learning · Collaborative decision-making

1 Introduction

In the modern technological environment, the complexity of collaborative decision-making is increasingly rising, particularly in systems that require multi-party involvement and highly dynamic responses. As an advanced machine learning technique, multi-agent reinforcement learning (MARL) addresses this challenge through the interaction and self-improvement of distributed agents [1]. These agents not only learn to make optimal decisions in changing environments but also collaborate to achieve common goals, which has been proven valuable in fields such as intelligent traffic systems and automated production lines [2]. However, despite the theoretical and experimental success of multi-agent systems, they still face a range of challenges in real-world applications, such as strategy integration, resource allocation, and real-time responsiveness [3]. To address

R. Xu et al. (Eds.): ICCC 2024, LNCS 15426, pp. 107–115, 2025.
https://doi.org/10.1007/978-3-031-77954-1_7

these issues, the introduction of new algorithmic optimization methods and improved collaboration mechanisms can further expand their application prospects in industrial, economic, and social management domains.

2 Theoretical Foundations of MARL

2.1 Definition and Classification of Multi-agent Systems

A Multi-Agent System (MAS) consists of multiple interacting agents, each capable of autonomous decision-making, able to perform tasks and solve problems in a given environment. These agents can be software agents, robots, or other entities with automated decision-making functions. In an MAS, agents respond to environmental states to achieve their respective goals, which may involve cooperation or competition.

Competitive agents have conflicting goals, where the success of one agent often comes at the expense of others. In cooperative systems, all agents share the same goal, working together to achieve a common final objective.

Hybrid agents collaborate under certain conditions and compete under others. For example, in e-commerce markets, sellers may compete on prices but collaborate to set standards to ensure market stability [4].

2.2 Core Concepts of Reinforcement Learning

Reinforcement Learning (RL) is a branch of machine learning that enables agents to learn how to maximize cumulative rewards through interaction with their environment, as shown in Fig. 1.

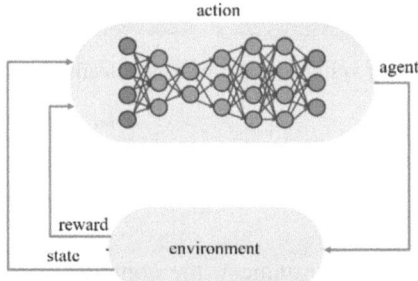

Fig. 1. Reinforcement learning foundation model.

Agents use trial and error to discover the relationship between actions and rewards without predefined rules. RL's key feature is its ability to handle long-term goals in decision-making processes, making it suitable for problems ranging from simple to highly complex.

2.3 Characteristics of Multi-agent Reinforcement Learning

In MAS, the large number of agents and the continuous evolution of their strategies create a highly non-static environment. Changes in one agent's behavior affect the decision-making environment of others, significantly increasing system dynamics. The complexity of MAS introduces uncertainty into the learning process. Agents must make decisions in environments with incomplete information, and their decisions depend on each other, which increases the difficulty of converging on optimal strategies during learning.

Designing effective communication and coordination mechanisms to ensure that agents' strategies can work in collaboration is a core challenge in MARL. In cooperative tasks, agents need to learn how to share information and allocate tasks to achieve optimal collective performance.

3 Application Cases of MARL in Collaborative Decision-Making

3.1 Application in Intelligent Traffic Systems

As urbanization accelerates, traffic congestion has become a major challenge for cities around the world. The goal of Intelligent Traffic Systems (ITS) is to reduce congestion and improve road utilization by optimizing traffic signal control and route scheduling [5]. The application of Multi-Agent Reinforcement Learning (MARL) in such systems focuses on dynamically adjusting traffic signals and coordinating multiple traffic nodes to optimize flow distribution.

In a specific application, a city's traffic management system is designed as a multi-agent system, where each traffic signal acts as an agent, capable of independently adjusting its decisions based on real-time traffic data. These agents use the Q-learning algorithm to update their strategies, aiming to minimize wait times and vehicle queues at specific intersections. Through information sharing among agents, the entire system can coordinate traffic lights over a wider range to optimize traffic flow across the city.

After deploying the MARL system, the average vehicle waiting time and overall delay at major intersections have been greatly reduced. A comparison of key performance indicators before and after implementation is shown in Table 1.

Table 1. Comparison of Key Performance Indicators for Intelligent Traffic System

Indicator	Before Deployment	After Deployment	Improvement Percentage
Average Waiting Time (seconds)	120	80	33.33%
Average Vehicle Delay (seconds)	300	180	40%
Traffic Handling Capacity (vehicles/hour)	2000	2700	35%

3.2   Collaborative Robots in Automated Manufacturing

In modern automated manufacturing, the design and implementation of collaborative robot systems are crucial for improving production efficiency and reducing costs. Traditional production lines typically consist of independently operating robots, each performing specific tasks with limited interaction and collaboration capabilities [6]. This setup restricts the flexibility and adaptability of the production line, especially when faced with complex manufacturing tasks.

MARL offers a solution by enabling robots to learn how to collaborate effectively in various operating environments, thereby optimizing the entire production process. In a typical application scenario, an automotive parts manufacturer uses MARL to optimize its welding and assembly lines. Each robot is treated as an agent, capable of automatically adjusting its task execution strategy based on real-time production data. For example, welding robots can dynamically adjust their welding sequence and speed according to the progress of assembly robots, maximizing the overall efficiency of the production line. This setup allows the entire production line to respond more flexibly to order changes, reducing time wasted due to waiting or unnecessary operations.

After deploying the MARL system, the production efficiency of the welding and assembly lines improved, and costs significantly decreased. A comparison of key performance indicators before and after the introduction of the collaborative robot system is shown in Table 2.

Table 2. Comparison of Key Performance Indicators for Collaborative Robot System

Indicator	Before deployment	After deployment	Improvement percentage
Overall Production Efficiency (%)	75	90	20%
Average Production Time (hours/unit)	3	2.4	20%
Downtime Due to Failures (hours/month)	50	30	40%
Production Increase (%)	0	15	15%

4   Optimization Strategies for MARL

4.1   Algorithm Optimization

Policy gradient methods are techniques that directly optimize strategies, allowing agents to adjust their strategy parameters using gradient ascent to maximize cumulative rewards. In multi-agent environments, policy gradient methods are particularly useful because they help agents learn how to collaborate or compete without needing an explicit environmental model. For example, using off-policy gradient techniques, agents can learn from the experiences of other agents, accelerating the learning process and improving overall system efficiency [7], as shown in Fig. 2.

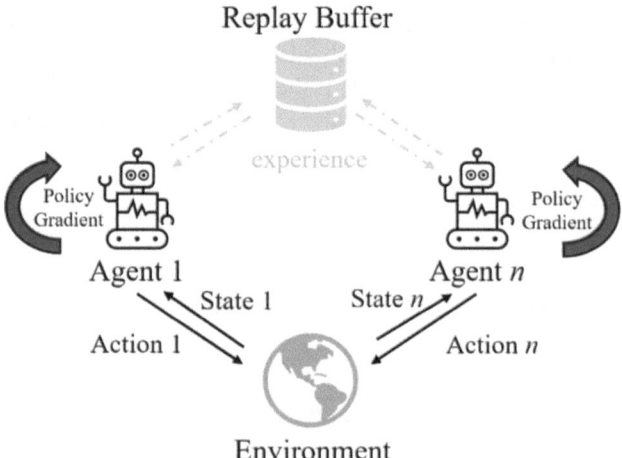

Fig. 2. Algorithm Structure Diagram

Deep reinforcement learning combines deep learning with reinforcement learning, enabling agents to process high-dimensional sensory inputs and make complex decisions. In multi-agent systems, deep reinforcement learning can be used to analyze complex data from multiple agents, allowing each agent to recognize and adapt to the strategies of other agents. For example, Deep Q-Networks (DQN) have been extended to Multi-Agent Deep Deterministic Policy Gradient (MADDPG), allowing agents to simultaneously optimize and coordinate their actions during training.

4.2 Innovation in Collaboration Mechanisms

In multi-agent reinforcement learning systems, designing effective reward mechanisms is key to promoting agent collaboration. Traditional reward mechanisms typically reward individual agents based on their performance, but in multi-agent environments, this method may lead to competition rather than cooperation. To solve this problem, researchers have designed shared reward mechanisms, where agents are rewarded not only for their own behavior but also based on the overall performance of the group. This method encourages agents to seek strategies that benefit the entire system, rather than just themselves [8].

Strategy coordination is a core issue in multi-agent systems, especially in complex dynamic environments. To optimize collaboration, a technique called "strategy sharing" was developed, allowing agents to share their strategies and experiences in real-time, thereby coordinating their action plans. This technique is implemented through a central communication node, where each agent uploads its predictions and decisions, then receives information from other agents. This real-time information exchange significantly improves collaboration efficiency and response speed.

5 Experiments

5.1 Experimental Setup

Reservoir Group Optimization is a complex four-reservoir system proposed by Larson [9], which is mainly used for hydropower generation and irrigation, as shown in Fig. 3, where Q_i is the inflow of the reservoir, S_i is the amount of water stored in the reservoir, and Re_i is the discharge of the reservoir, and $i = 1,2,3,4$ represents the four reservoirs.

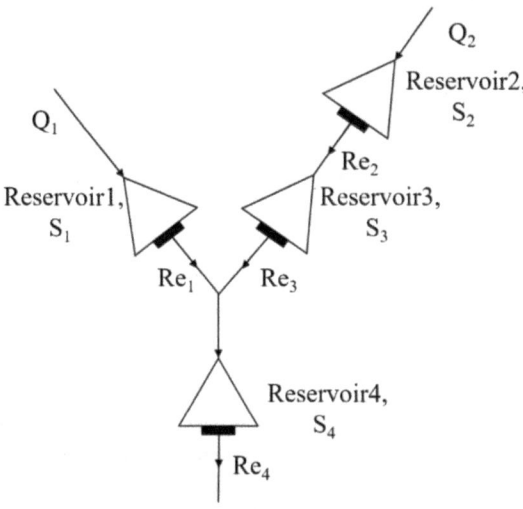

Fig. 3. Four-reservoir system

The operation of each reservoir is constrained by seasonal flood control needs, and all reservoir releases generate electricity through turbines, and the goal of reservoir cluster joint merit scheduling optimization is to maximize the total benefit of the system during the operation period of 12-time steps, as shown in Table 3.

5.2 Experimental Results

Figure 4 illustrates the comparison of power generation benefits between single-agent and multi-agent systems, with a total of 100,000 iterations and evaluations conducted every 50 iterations. As shown in the figure, the multi-agent algorithm achieves near-optimal reservoir scheduling solutions in fewer iterations, demonstrating superior computational efficiency compared to the single-agent algorithm.

Table 3. Relevant parameters of the four-reservoir system

Data	Reservoir	Time step											
		1	2	3	4	5	6	7	8	9	10	11	12
Power generation benefits	1	1.1	1	1	1.2	1.8	2.5	2.2	2	1.8	2.2	1.8	1.4
	2	1.4	1.1	1	1	1.2	1.8	2.5	2.2	2	1.8	2.2	1.8
	3	1	1	1.2	1.8	2.5	2.2	2	1.8	2.2	1.8	1.4	1.1
	4	2.6	2.9	3.6	4.4	4.2	4	3.8	4.1	3.6	3.1	2.7	2.5
Inflow of reservoirs	1	2	2	2	2	2	2	2	2	2	2	2	2
	2	3	3	3	3	3	3	3	3	3	3	3	3
	3	0	0	0	0	0	0	0	0	0	0	0	0
	4	0	0	0	0	0	0	0	0	0	0	0	0
Maximum water storage	1	10	10	10	10	10	10	10	10	10	10	10	10
	2	10	10	10	10	10	10	10	10	10	10	10	10
	3	10	10	10	10	10	10	10	10	10	10	10	10
	4	15	15	15	15	15	15	15	15	15	15	15	15

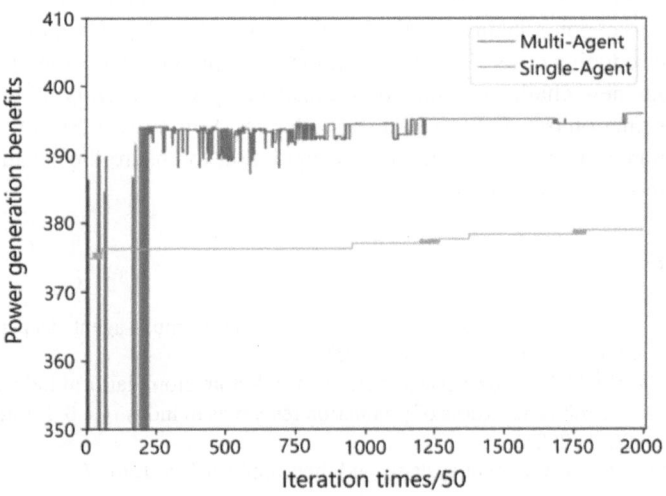

Fig. 4. Comparison of power generation benefits

According to Fig. 5, compared to single-agent algorithms, multi-agent algorithms improve the overall benefits of hydropower generation by coordinating the competitive relationships between different reservoirs through controlled downstream flow.

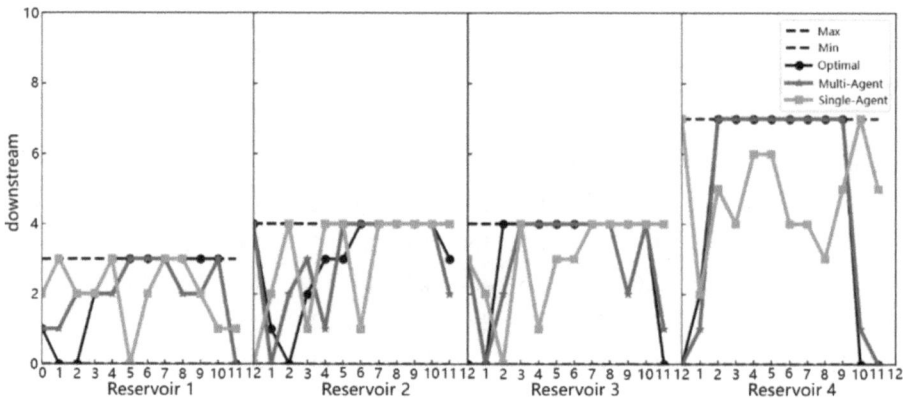

Fig. 5. Comparison of scheduling schemes

6   Conclusions and Outlook

Multi-agent reinforcement learning technology has demonstrated its excellent capability in handling complex and dynamic environments, especially in applications such as intelligent traffic systems and automated manufacturing, showing great potential for improving efficiency and decision quality. As the technology matures and receives policy support, the market potential in these fields will further expand, particularly in improving efficiency and reducing costs [10]. However, the widespread application of this technology also brings new challenges, including ensuring system stability and dealing with complex coordination issues. Facing these challenges, future research and practice need to strike a balance between innovation and regulation to ensure the sustainability and ethics of technological development.

References

1. Oroojlooy, A., Hajinezhad, D.: A review of cooperative multi-agent deep reinforcement learning. Appl. Intell. **53**, 13677–13722 (2023)
2. Seitz, M., Gehlhoff, F., Cruz Salazar, L.A., et al.: Automation platform independent multi-agent system for robust networks of production resources in industry 4.0. J. Intell. Manufact. **32**(7), 2023–2041 (2021)
3. Xie, J., Liu, C.C.: Multi-agent systems and their applications. J. Int. Coun. Elec. Eng. **7**(1), 188–197 (2017)
4. Luo, A., Ma, H., Ren, H., et al.: Estimator-based reinforcement learning consensus control for multiagent systems with discontinuous constraints. IEEE Trans. Neural Netw. Learn. Syst. (2024)
5. Yang, S., Yang, B., Zeng, Z., et al.: Causal inference multi-agent reinforcement learning for traffic signal control. Inf. Fus. **94**, 243–256 (2023)
6. Zhu, Y., Xiao, M., Robbins, D., et al.: Walking representation and simulation based on multi-source image fusion and multi-agent reinforcement learning for gait rehabilitation. Artif. Intell. Med. **156**, 102945 (2024)
7. Yuan, Q.: Residential demand response online optimization based on multi-agent deep reinforcement learning. Elec. Power Syst. Res. **237**, 110987 (2024)

8. Dong, S., Li, C., Yang, S., et al.: Decentralized counterfactual value with threat detection for multi-agent reinforcement learning in mixed cooperative and competitive environments. Expert Syst. Appl. **257**, 125116 (2024)
9. Larson, R.E.: State Increment Dynamic Programming. Elsevier, New York (1968)
10. Xu, B., Luan, W., Yang, J., et al.: Integrated three-stage decentralized scheduling for virtual power plants: a model-assisted multi-agent reinforcement learning method. Appl. Ener. **376**(PA), 123985 (2024)

LLM-Based Automating Product Information Retrieval for Industry Analysis: A Real-World Application

Chen Liao[1,2], Gang Cheng[1,2], Shilei Huang[1,2], and Lin Yao[1(✉)]

[1] IMSL Shenzhen Key Lab, PKU-HKUST Shenzhen Hong Kong Institution,
ShenZhen, China
yaolin@imsl.org.cn
[2] Shenzhen Raisound Technologies, Co., Ltd., ShenZhen, China

Abstract. In the rapidly evolving digital landscape, effective retrieval of product information from enterprise websites is crucial for enterprise research, industry analysis, and strategic planning, which rely on accurate and comprehensive data. In this context, a "product" is defined as any tangible item, a solution, or a service. This paper proposes a novel method for extracting such product data-such as product name, category, description, and specifications-directly from company websites. Our approach leverages the capabilities of Large Language Models (LLMs) to enhance the accuracy and automation of the web-page information retrieval process. The adoption of LLMs allows for a more sophisticated extraction and organization of data, overcoming the limitations of conventional methods. Currently, there is a notable absence of open-source or commercial databases that comprehensively cover enterprise products, making it challenging to conduct comparative studies. Our proposed method aims to fill this gap, providing a tool for gathering product information that can be used to assess competitive differences.

Keywords: Large Language Model · Information Retrieval · Product Information

1 Introduction

In the current digital era, accurate and comprehensive product information is crucial in making informed decisions. In this context, a "product" is defined as follows: 1) a tangible item refers to a physical object or good that can be touched and utilized, such as machinery, consumer electronics, or industrial equipment; or, 2) a solution refers to a comprehensive set of tools or systems designed to address specific needs or problems faced by other companies, which may include

1. Supported by Shenzhen Science and Technology Program (No:GJHZ20220913144 201002).
2. Supported by IER Foundation 2022(IERF202203).

software, technological systems, or consulting services; or, 3) a service involves intangible offerings that provide value through specialized expertise or support, such as maintenance services, or professional advisory services.

For industry analysts working in financial institutions and government agencies, access to detailed product data across various enterprises is essential for conducting enterprise research, industry analysis, and strategic planning. However, such a comprehensive database does not currently exist in China, resulting in a time-consuming analysis process for analysts. Furthermore, given that this is a real-world application, analysts are particularly interested in high-tech industries such as semiconductors and renewable energy. Companies in these sectors typically do not list their products on e-commerce platforms, rendering existing e-commerce product information retrieval methods inapplicable. Additionally, some enterprises operate in international markets and only have English-language websites, which poses a challenge for analysts conducting the analysis.

Obtaining product information from enterprises' websites and organize into structured data present significant challenges: 1) Enterprise websites vary widely in their structure, design, and the way they present product information; 2) Product information may presents in a more unstructured or inconsistent manner.

With the emergence of Large Language Models (LLMs), domain and application specialization has become a critical focus in their development [7,10,16]. Meanwhile, some researchers are conducting detailed analyses on the practical applications of LLMs in real-world scenarios [4,9,17,19]. Motivated by these observations and real-world demands, we propose a novel approach that leverages LLMs for product information retrieval from web pages.

The main contributions of this paper are: 1) We propose a novel method that leverages a LLM for a real-world application, with different prompting techniques, demonstrating the true potential of LLMs in addressing practical challenges; 2) Our approach is entirely training-free, relying solely on the latent capabilities of LLMs, offers a valuable reference for application in other domains; 3) Our solution has been shown to closely approximate human understandings.

2   Related Works

Information retrieval (IR) systems aims to retrieve information via user query, including various types of information such as text, audio, images, and so on. In our context, we focus on HTML Document Object Model (DOM) tree, which is semi-structured text contents. In the past few years, web-page-based information retrieval can be divided into three categories: 1) text-based solution, 2) visual-based solution and 3) multi-modal solution.

Text-based solutions typically refer to natural language processing (NLP) solutions. Some researchers adopted deep-learning algorithms such as train a model base on Transformers [13], with advanced techniques such as self-designed attention patterns [15], diving into the latent semantic information [5], multi-feature fusion [14], and unsupervised entity extraction [3]; while the other researchers employed Conditional random fields (CRF) and nondeterministic finite automaton (NFA) [12]. Other researchers proposed visual-based solution [6] transforms the complex task of text extraction into a web-page object detection problem, effectively bypassing the need for DOM tree processing. Multi-modal solutions fully utilize the visual information contained in a web-page [8,18], while other researchers [1,11] also supports non-text contents retrieval.

In comparison to the aforementioned works, our method demonstrates greater extensibility for similar web-based information retrieval tasks. It is more flexible and does not necessitate extensive labor for data labeling, leveraging the capabilities of large language models (LLMs) instead.

3   Approach

In this section, we break down our approach into four key components, delving into the details, the prompting techniques, and the interactions between these components:

– Data Preparation: Given that we are working with a semi-structured DOM tree, we prepare the data by removing unnecessary HTML content.
– Website Classification: We classify the web pages into three distinct categories: product detail pages, product category pages, and others.
– Product Tree Construction: This component enables the construction of a clear, noise-free representation of the product structure.
– Product Detail Retrieval: In this final step, we retrieve product names, descriptions, and specifications (when available) to enable industry analysts to perform detailed comparisons of specific products.

3.1   Data Preparation

To retrieve information from enterprise homepages, we used an in-house developed web crawler to gather the web pages. Considering the characteristics of product pages, we limited the crawling depth to 3 - each hyperlink leading to a new internal page is considered to represent one level of navigation-as some enterprises have forums or external links that could lead to infinite crawling. We then removed all comments and footers that were irrelevant to our analysis.

Lastly, we eliminated unnecessary HTML tags-such as `<div>`, `<a>`, and `<script>`-which do not convey structural information, while retaining tags like `<table>`, `<ul>`, and `<li>`, which provide meaningful structural details. Additionally, we compared each child page with the homepage and removed nodes that shared identical text or XPath, such as those within `<footer>` and `<copyright>` tags. As shown in Fig. 1, this process significantly reduces noise in the webpages and preserves the meaningful information.

Fig. 1. Example of Data Preparation Result: The green section indicates the content retained after data preparation, while the red parts will be removed. (Color figure online)

3.2   Website Classification

In general, an enterprise's website encompasses a wide range of information, including company introductions, news, products, honors, and more. Our primary focus is on pages that contain product-related information. However, it is challenging to ascertain whether a given page contains product information based solely on easily accessible properties such as the page URL, title, and similar metadata.

Therefore, the first step in our approach is to classify the web pages into distinct categories. We define three categories: (1) Product Detail Pages (PDP), which provide an in-depth description of a single product; (2) Product Category Pages (PCP), which present multiple products, typically including product names and sometimes brief descriptions; and (3) Other Pages (OP), which cover content related to honors, employment, organizational information, and similar topics. Below is a sample of the system prompt we used:

System Prompt:
You must carefully consider the categories and their corresponding explanations below to determine which category this webpage belongs to.
   - Other
   Explanation: This page primarily contains content such as news, company profiles, job postings, client introductions, contact information, or tenders, and is not directly related to products, services, or solutions.
   - Product Category Page
   Explanation: This page simply lists the names of products, services, or solutions.
   - Product Detail Page
   Explanation: This page contains detailed information about a specific product, service, or solution, describing it in depth.
   Note: You only need to return the name of the category, and you can only respond with one of the categories provided above.

To ensure that the LLM fully comprehends the task, we structure the prompt into three distinct components: (1) a concise introduction to the task, clearly stating the primary objective-in this case, identifying the appropriate category; (2) a detailed list of category names accompanied by comprehensive explanations of each category to provide clear definitions; and (3) a specification of the desired output format, which in this instance is limited to the 'category name' alone.

As a result, the product category pages (PCPs) will contribute to Product Tree Construction step, while product detail pages (PDPs) will contribute to Product Detail Retrieval.

3.3   Product Tree Construction

A Product Tree is a semi-structured output that is difficult for large language models (LLMs) to interpret from plain text alone. To address this, we employed the technique of Few-Shot restrictive prompting [2] to introduce in-context learning, ensure the LLM produces the desired results. In our prompt, we divided the tree-building process into two stages: (1) constructing the product tree and (2) refining the product tree.

The product tree constructed at this stage is a basic product tree (BPT), as it is built using product category pages (PCP), which typically do not include exact product names but only the broader categories. Our ultimate objective is to develop an advanced product tree (APT) that incorporates specific product names. The APT serves as a structured framework that provides a systematic representation of an enterprise's product offerings. This model enables analysts to quickly obtain a comprehensive overview of the enterprise's portfolio, facilitating efficient analysis and decision-making. The APT will be completed in next section.

Below is an example of the prompt for building the BPT, as well as the BPT generated by LLM.

System Prompt to Build BPT:
Your responsibility is to parse the semi-structures and text, and to construct a tree structure.
The term "product" is defined as anything that is used and consumed by individuals, satisfying a certain need or desire. This includes both tangible goods and intangible services.
The following is an example, marked by `<example>` and `</example>` to indicate the beginning and end of the example.
`<example>`
  EXAMPLE OF BASIC PRODUCT TREE
`</example>`
Output:
- Product Center
  - Processor Chips
  - About Us
  - Product Solutions
    - Distributed Storage Systems
    - Database Appliances
  - Industry Applications
    - Intelligent Computing Centers
    - EDA Storage
    - Finance
  - Software
  - Organization

To ensure the retrieval of product information exclusively, we emphasize the definition of a product within the prompt and apply the Few-shot Prompting technique by including an example of the desired tree structure in the system prompt. Notably, we observed that the use of the markers `<example></example>` is essential for LLMs to recognize that the enclosed content is an example. Specifically, in cases where a webpage contains minimal product-related content or sparse textual content (dominated by HTML tags), the absence of these markers leads LLMs to overexert efforts in identifying 'product-related' content, often resulting in the output being the BPT provided in the prompt.

System Prompt to Refine BPT:

You are an advanced data cleansing tool tasked with removing content unrelated to 'products' from the provided tree structure.

The term "product" is defined as anything used and consumed by individuals that satisfies a certain need or desire, encompassing both tangible goods and intangible services.

You must rigorously evaluate each node within the tree structure to determine whether it pertains to 'products'.

Output:
- Product Center
  - Processor Chips
  - Product Solutions
    - Distributed Storage Systems
    - Database Appliances
  - Industry Applications
    - Intelligent Computing Centers
    - EDA Storage
    - Finance
  - Software

Additionally, we observed that, despite emphasizing the definition of 'product' in the prompt, there were instances where LLMs failed to accurately identify and extract product-related information exclusively. To address this issue, we introduced an additional step in our process: instructing the LLM to refine the generated tree structure by removing content that is irrelevant to products. This refinement step helps ensure that the final output focuses solely on product-related information.

3.4 Product Detail Retrieval

In the previous section, we developed a comprehensive and well-structured basic product tree (BPT) that provides a clear overview of the enterprise's product hierarchy. In this section, we aim to extract key information related to these products.

Guided by the interests of industry analysts, we identified five key types of information: product name, product category, product description, and, where applicable, product model and specifications. The information retrieval process is divided into three steps: (1) extracting the product name and basic product category (BPC), (2) utilizing a large language model (LLM) to place the product within the product tree, and (3) extracting the remaining relevant information. The process is shown in Fig. 2.

- Step 1: We designed an initial prompt that instructs the LLM to extract the product name and the Basic Product Category (BPC) based on a pre-processed, semi-structured webpage and the associated Basic Product Tree (BPT).
- Step 2: Utilizing the product name, BPT, and BPC, we formulated a well-structured prompt that enables the integration of the product into a pre-defined hierarchical tree. This approach allows us to identify the product category as defined by the enterprise, rather than relying on the LLM to deduce a category independently-a process that, while accurate, proves less beneficial for industry analysts. This step will yield a more specific product category characterized by a hierarchical relationship, rather than a simple categorical designation.
- Step 3: We provide the LLM with the semi-structured webpage, product name, and product category, instructing it to retrieve the product description. Where applicable, we also extract the product model and specifications, subsequently parsing the output into a structured format.

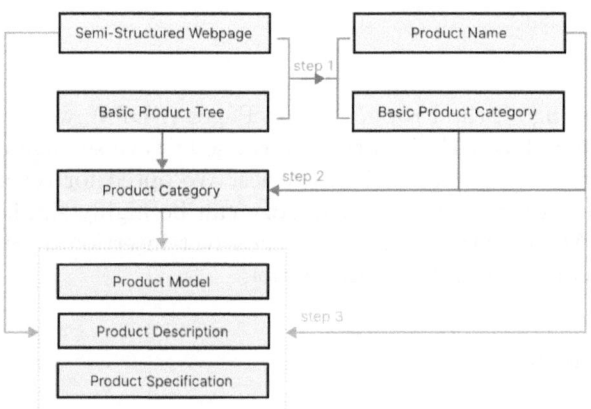

Fig. 2. Data Flow of Product Detail Retrieval

This process was iterated for all Product Detail Pages (PDPs). In Fig. 2, blue, purple and green lines and arrows shows corresponding data flow of Step 1 to Step 3. The boxes in light purple are the results of Product Detail Retrieval.

Table 1. Quantitative Evaluation Result

	Name	Category	Description	Model	Specification
Total	1449	1449	1449	823	849
R1	83.88	54.77	89.91	58.37	76.11
R2	73.98	48.18	81.25	54.90	73.19
RL	83.88	54.77	88.80	58.37	75.43
BLEU	87.52	66.08	88.57	58.08	69.20
Avg.	82.32	55.95	87.13	57.43	73.48

Table 2. Subjective Evaluation Result

	Name	Category	Description	Model	Specification
Total	145	145	145	82	85
C	4.58	4.18	4.78	3.76	4.26
F	5.00	4.75	5.00	4.00	3.97
U	4.73	4.45	4.70	4.14	4.54
Avg.	4.77	4.46	4.83	3.97	4.26

After processing all the Product Detail Pages (PDPs), we reconstructed the Advanced Product Tree (APT) of the enterprise by reverse-engineering based on the extracted product names and categories. We opted for reverse-engineering because products within a specific category can be highly similar, which could confuse the LLM, potentially leading to incorrect insertion in Step 2 and, consequently, inaccurate product categorization.

4   Experiments

4.1   Dataset and LLM

From the initial 500 enterprises of interest to industry analysts, we excluded those whose websites were inaccessible at the time of analysis and randomly selected 100 from the remaining 447 enterprises. Using an in-house developed web-crawler with a crawling depth of 3, we obtained a total of 11,274 pages. Under the supervision of industry analysts, we manually labeled the products, establishing this dataset as the ground truth for our evaluations. The final dataset comprises 1,449 products, where each product record is defined by a unique combination of product name, category, and description-each of which are required fields. Of these records, 823 include model information, and 849 include specifications, while the other products remain no model and specification information.

The LLM employed in our study is Doubao-32k-pro, developed by ByteDance. We selected this model due to its exceptional ability to follow instructions while maintaining a moderate level of natural language under-standing. This combination ensures that the model accurately comprehends the requirements specified in the prompt and reliably produces output in the desired format.

4.2   Evaluation

Given our objective to address a real-world issue, we incorporated both subjec-tive and quantitative evaluations in our study. While the quantitative metrics provide an objective measure of performance, the subjective evaluations offer valuable insights into the perceived quality and relevance of the output from the perspective of industry analysts.

4.2.1   Subjective Evaluation
In the subjective evaluation phase, each industry analyst independently selected a random sample comprising 10% of the total records. These samples were reviewed based on three key criteria: comprehensibility (C), fluency (F), and utility (U). The evaluation scale ranged from 0 to 5, where a score of 0 indicated that the record was completely meaningless, while a score of 5 signified that the record was perfectly accurate and highly useful. Three analysts conducted these evaluations independently. As illustrated in Table 2, the analysts expressed overall satisfaction with the results, particularly highlighting the accuracy and utility of the product name and description fields.

Subjectively, the analysts had differing perspectives on the results. Some analysts, who were already familiar with the products in the dataset, found the results to be sufficient even without precise details like product models and spec-ifications. In contrast, other analysts, who were less familiar with the products, placed a higher value on the accuracy of these specific details, as they relied on them to deepen their understanding of the products and to conduct thorough evaluations of the enterprises.

4.2.2   Quantitative Evaluation
Although our task is fundamentally an information retrieval (IR) task, the incor-poration of large language models (LLMs) in our approach has transformed it into a hybrid process, combining elements of both generation and retrieval. Consequently, the primary focus of our evaluation shifts towards assessing the textual similarity between the retrieved snippets and the labeled dataset. To provide a quantitative assessment of our approach, we employ different evalu-ation metrics across various categories of product information. Specifically, we utilize the BLEU score and the F1-scores of ROUGE-1 (R1), ROUGE-2 (R2), and ROUGE-L (RL) to rigorously evaluate the performance of our method.

As shown in Table 1, our method shows a good accuracy in product infor-mation retrieval. The high scores of product 'Description', 'Name' and 'Specifi-cation' indicates a strong alignment between the retrieved descriptions and the labeled data, suggesting that our approach performs particularly well in retrieving accurate and contextually relevant product descriptions, product names and product specifications. However, the score for the product 'Category' is notably lower than other fields. Upon analyzing the basic product categories (BPC) generated by the LLM, we observed that when explicit information regarding the product category is not readily available on the page, the LLM often tends to generate a category by inferring from the context rather than selecting the closest match from the basic product tree (BPT) provided in the prompt. Regarding the product "Model," during the data labeling stage, we made a strict distinction between the product name and the product model. However, in some cases, the product model is embedded within the product name, making it challenging for LLMs to accurately discern the boundary between the two.

These results indicate that while the approach is effective overall, there is room for improvement, particularly in the retrieval of category, model, and specification information.

5   Conclusion and Future Work

In this paper, we harness the capabilities of large language models (LLMs) to address a real-world challenge. We propose an LLM-based automated approach for retrieving product information from enterprise websites, aimed at assisting industry analysts in conducting competitive research and analyzing industry development trends. Our process begins with an in-house developed crawler that systematically gathers web pages from enterprise websites. These pages are then classified, followed by the construction of product trees, enabling the extraction of relevant product information. To evaluate the effectiveness of our approach, we utilized a self-labeled dataset, curated under the supervision of industry analysts. The results demonstrate that our approach successfully retrieves accurate product information, validating its effectiveness for real-world application.

While our work demonstrates a practical solution to a real-world problem, there are still several avenues for further enhancement to increase the precision and comprehensiveness of the retrieved product information. For instance, integrating optical character recognition (OCR) could enable the extraction of textual data embedded within images, thereby enriching the dataset with information that might otherwise be overlooked. Additionally, expanding the scope of the information retrieved to include elements such as product images and user manuals would provide a more holistic view of the products.

Moreover, the methodology developed in this study has potential applications beyond product information retrieval. It could be adapted to other forms of enterprise data extraction, such as tracking corporate news, monitoring enterprise events, or analyzing investor relations. This transferability underscores the broader utility of our approach in addressing various information retrieval challenges across different sectors.

References

1. Alarte, J., Silva, J.: Page-level main content extraction from heterogeneous web-pages. ACM Trans. Knowl. Discov. Data **15**(6) (2021). https://doi.org/10.1145/3451168
2. Arora, S., et al.: Ask me anything: a simple strategy for prompting language models. In: The Eleventh International Conference on Learning Representations (2023). https://openreview.net/forum?id=bhUPJnS2g0X
3. Dalvi, B.B., Cohen, W.W., Callan, J.: In: WebSets: extracting sets of entities from the web using unsupervised information extraction. In: WSDM 2012, pp. 243–252. Association for Computing Machinery, New York (2012). https://doi.org/10.1145/2124295.2124327
4. Huang, Y., et al.: Large language models for networking: applications, enabling techniques, and challenges. IEEE Netw. (2024)
5. Joby, P.P.: Expedient information retrieval system for web pages using the natural language modeling. J. Artif. Intell. Capsule Netw. **2**(2), 100–110 (2020)
6. Kumar, A., Morabia, K., Wang, J., Chang, K.C.C., Schwing, A.: Cova: context-aware visual attention for webpage information extraction. arXiv (2021). https://doi.org/10.48550/arXiv.2110.12320
7. Ling, C., et al.: Domain specialization as the key to make large language models disruptive: a comprehensive survey (2024). https://arxiv.org/abs/2305.18703
8. Liu, J., Lin, L., Cai, Z., Wang, J., Kim, H.J.: Deep web data extraction based on visual information processing. J. Ambient Intell. Humanized Comput. **15**(2) (2024)
9. Ozkaya, I.: Application of large language models to software engineering tasks: opportunities, risks, and implications. IEEE Softw. **40**(3), 4–8 (2023)
10. Patil, R., Gudivada, V.: A review of current trends, techniques, and challenges in large language models (llms). Appl. Sci. **14**(5) (2024). https://www.mdpi.com/2076-3417/14/5/2074
11. Ramalingam, M., Saranya, D., ShankarRam, R., Chinnasamy, P., Ramprathap, K., Kalaiarasi, A.: An automated framework for dynamic web information retrieval using deep learning. In: 2022 International Conference on Computer Communication and Informatics (ICCCI), pp. 1–6 (2022)
12. Shaukat, K., Masood, N., Khushi, M.: A novel approach to data extraction on hyperlinked webpages. Appl. Sci. **9**(23) (2019). https://www.mdpi.com/2076-3417/9/23/5102
13. Vaswani, A.: Attention is all you need. In: Advances in Neural Information Processing Systems (2017)
14. Wang, C., Wei, P.: A novel web page text information extraction method. In: 2019 IEEE 3rd Information Technology, Networking, Electronic and Automation Control Conference (ITNEC), pp. 2213–2218 (2019)
15. Wang, Q., Fang, Y., Ravula, A., Feng, F., Quan, X., Liu, D.: Webformer: the web-page transformer for structure information extraction. In: Proceedings of the ACM Web Conference 2022, pp. 3124–3133. Association for Computing Machinery, New York (2022). https://doi.org/10.1145/3485447.3512032
16. Yang, J., et al.: Harnessing the power of llms in practice: a survey on chatgpt and beyond. ACM Trans. Knowl. Discov. Data **18**(6), 1–32 (2024)
17. Yang, R., Tan, T.F., Lu, W., Thirunavukarasu, A.J., Ting, D.S.W., Liu, N.: Large language models in health care: development, applications, and challenges. Health Care Sci. **2**(4), 255–263 (2023). https://onlinelibrary.wiley.com/doi/abs/10.1002/hcs2.61

18. Zhang, M., Yang, Z., Ali, S., Ding, W.: Web page information extraction service based on graph convolutional neural network and multimodal data fusion. In: 2021 IEEE International Conference on Web Services (ICWS), pp. 681–687 (2021)
19. Zhou, H., et al.: Large language model (llm) for telecommunications: a comprehensive survey on principles, key techniques, and opportunities (2024). https://arxiv.org/abs/2405.10825

Author Index

R. Xu et al. (Eds.): ICCC 2024, LNCS 15426, p. 129, 2025.
https://doi.org/10.1007/978-3-031-77954-1